John Scally

A BRAVE NEW WORLD?

VERITAS

First published 1998 by
Veritas Publications
7-8 Lower Abbey Street
Dublin 1

Copyright © John Scally 1998

ISBN 1 85390 309 4

British Library Cataloguing
in Publication Data.
A catalogue record for
this book is available
from the British Library.

Cover design by Barbara Croatto
Cover photograph of DNA double helix copyright © The Slide
File, Dublin. Reproduced with permission.
Printed in the Republic of Ireland by Betaprint Ltd, Dublin

To the memory of my Father

CONTENTS

ACKNOWLEDGMENTS

I would like to thank Professor David McConnell and Dr Tony Kavanagh of the Genetics Department in Trinity College, Monsignor Francis Donnelly of Drogheda, Tom Cooney of the Irish Council of Civil Liberties and Clare O'Grady Walshe for sharing their insights on the genetics revolution with me.

Special thanks to Dick Warner for encouraging my interest in genetics and for other kindnesses.

I am grateful to Professor Bill Shannon and Professor Tom O'Dowd for encouraging my interest in medical ethics.

My thanks also to Paul Tighe, Bernard Hoose and Rachel Iredale for their constructive suggestions.

I am indebted to Fr Sean Melody, Fiona Biggs, Maura Hyland, Brian Lynch and all at Veritas for their help and encouragement.

GLOSSARY OF TERMS

1. Amino acid: the building-blocks from which all proteins are made. Twenty different sorts occur naturally.

2. Chromosome: Humans have twenty-three pairs of chromosomes carrying their entire genetic specification.

3. DNA (deoxyribonucleic acid): in most living things, DNA is the molecule carrying primary genetic information. It consists of long chains of nucleotides, each of which is a base linked to a sugar (deoxyribose) and phosphate molecule.

4. Double helix: The three-dimensional structure of DNA in which two strands twist together in a spiral.

5. Gene: the unit of inheritance, consisting of a sequence of bases of DNA occupying a specific position within the genome.

6. Gene therapy: the deliberate repair or replacement of damaged genes.

7. Genome: the full set of chromosomes – essentially all the genes in an organism's DNA.

8. *in vitro*: in a test-tube

9. *in vivo*: in a living organism

10. Polygenic: controlled by or associated with more than one gene.

11. Transgenic: an organism containing genetic material artifically inserted from another species.

12. Virus: a sub-microscopic organism which has to invade another cell to replicate itself.

INTRODUCTION
SHALL WE PLAY GOD?

The two great constants of human existence – birth and death – were for centuries a matter for God and nature only. Now science has intervened. The news that a fifty-nine-year-old woman gave birth to twins on Christmas Day 1993 and the suggestion within a fortnight that eggs from aborted foetuses be used to restore the ovarian function in sterile woman to create babies prompted a tidal wave of comment – some of it illuminating; much of it not. The ghost of Frankenstein was regularly invoked and terms like 'womb-robbing' were bandied about.

At one stage in America a popular T-shirt carried a picture of an angst-ridden woman with a hand raised to her face in alarm. The bubble over her head read: 'Oh my God! I forgot to have children.' With the advent of people like Italian doctor, Professor Severino Antinori, such women now have the means to correct this omission. Antinori first came to public attention in October 1988 through his involvement in the 'brother-son' story – when he successfully took an ovary from a forty-eight-year-old woman, fertilised it with the sperm of her lover, and then implanted it in the womb of her daughter by a previous marriage. Even more controversial was Antinori's alleged involvement in the case of a sixty-one-year-old Sicilian widow who gave birth in 1993 after being reportedly impregnated with the frozen sperm of her late husband, who had died seven years earlier. He claims his pioneering work in the area of IVF for women who have passed the menopause has helped over a thousand couples to become parents.

1993 also saw another controversy with the establishment of a 'designer baby' service in a London gender clinic where couples who are desperate to have a baby of a particular sex can receive 'assistance' – although there is not a 100 per cent guarantee that the outcome will be a baby of the sex they choose. This development raises serious questions about the manipulation of gender and brings the process of childbearing, to some extent at least, into the area of quality control. The clinic has imposed restrictions on the treatment, for example it does not make its services available to couples who already have a boy and a girl, or have none at all, and is not party to abortions if the sex selection process is not a success.

1994 opened with yet further controversies in medical ethics over the case of a black mother who gave birth to a white baby and the possible use of eggs from aborted human foetuses to restore the ovarian function in sterile women and enable them to become pregnant. (When a female baby is born, her ovaries contain a lifetime's supply of eggs – perhaps as many as a million. Although they are immature, it may be possible to allow these eggs to grow to viability.) The technique, which has been used successfully in mice, aims to overcome the shortage of human eggs for 'test tube babies', and involves growing immature eggs from the aborted foetus until they are ready for fertilisation and implantation in their new mother's womb. One huge problem which this process would create is the psychological effects on the children when they are informed that their 'physiological mother' has been 'disposed of'.

On 5 October 1992 a young pregnant German woman on her way home from work drove her car into a tree, smashing her skull.

The woman was flown to hospital and put on life support. Doctors found that she was brain dead but when they sought permission from her parents for organ donation it was refused. The doctors then attempted to keep her body alive until the following year, when they hoped to deliver her child by Caesarean section. Nobody knew who the father was, and he never came forward. The woman's parents agreed to this suggestion, although they later claimed that they consented only under pressure from doctors. On 16 November 1992 the foetus spontaneously aborted and died. Sections of the German media criticised the doctor's actions, seeing it as a grisly experiment that destroyed the dignity of the woman's death, and called for tighter controls on clinical practice.

Cases such as these have generated much public anxiety that medical science has gone too far and that humankind has taken on powers hitherto reserved to God. The recent spectacular advances in genetics have fuelled this anxiety. Historically, medical ethics has always lagged behind developments in medical technology. Since its inception it has been a reactive discipline. To serve society adequately it must in the future take more of a lead – anticipating questions which are likely to arise. While genetic advances will in the future bring many life-enhancing possibilities they will also bring critical ethical questions. This book will examine many of them.

1
IF IT'S DNA IT'S OJ

Blessed Oliver Plunkett, The Elephant Man, OJ Simpson and a champion dog. At first glance this disparate quartet might seem an unlikely foursome; however, they are linked by one common factor – DNA testing.

St Peter's Church in Drogheda houses the head of Oliver Plunkett, a bishop who came to Ireland in penal times in 1870. As one of only two Catholic bishops at the time he had a price on his head. He was arrested and transported to England, convicted wrongly for his part in a plot to bring the French to Ireland, and was hanged, drawn, quartered and decapitated. His head was taken by his friends and put in a 'round tin box' and his forearms put in a 'long tin box'. The rest of his body was buried in the cemetery of St Giles outside London. His fellow prisoner, a Benedictine priest, was released in 1683, and he brought the head to Rome to Cardinal Howard, whom Plunkett had known in London before he came to Ireland. The Cardinal kept the head in Rome before sending it back to Plunkett's second successor in Drogheda where it was entrusted to the care of Sister Catherine Plunkett, herself a relative of Oliver.

In the interim the Benedictine priest had Oliver's body exhumed, probably illegally, and sent to a Benedictine monastery in Germany. Some time later it was returned to the Benedictine monastery in England. In 1975 six large portions of his body were returned to Drogheda. As there had been so much movement of his body parts it was decided to make a scientific investigation into whether or not the head and the relics belonged to the same person. Samples were taken surgically from the head and the relic with long needles and put into a container, carefully labelled and sent to the genetic laboratory in Tampa, Florida. The samples will be compared with samples taken from one of Plunkett's living relatives. Scientists dealing with the case face two problems in assessing the samples. Firstly, the original samples may not be pure enough because they have been subjected to a great deal of handling during their travels. Secondly, the DNA may be too scarce. DNA detectives are also currently working on the mask of the Elephant Man.

The use of science in crime detection and investigation has been going on since the fictional days of Sherlock Holmes. In 1902, in Paris, in a landmark case in the history of crime detection, a leading French detective, Alfonse Bertillon, secured a conviction on the basis of a fingerprint left by the killer at the scene of the crime. This was the first time a fingerprint had been used as evidence of identity. The idea came from ancient Japan, where a finger pressed into a clay pot identified the potter. In 1985 two young girls were killed near the Leicestershire village of Narborough. This time the murderer was tracked down because of his 'DNA fingerprint' which is as much a statement of personal uniqueness as an actual fingerprint. With the OJ Simpson case genetic evidence took central stage. As was apparent in the discussion of the Fr Michael Cleary and Ross Hamilton controversy, DNA evidence is increasingly used in cases where paternity is disputed.

In the infamous OJ Simpson trial much of the case centred on

DNA. Hence the slogan: If it's DNA it's OJ. His defence team initially tried to block Los Angeles prosecutors from presenting DNA evidence they believed incriminated the former football star in the June 1994 murders of his ex-wife Nicole Brown Simpson and her friend Ronald Goldman – playing up the controversies surrounding DNA profiling during a pre-trial admissibility hearing. In several cases, while courts have upheld the validity of DNA profiling in general they have thrown out the results of particular tests as flawed.

The defence made much of the so-called Frye Standard, whereby in Californian courts attorneys must establish that the scientific evidence they wish to present is generally accepted by the scientific community. Simpson's lawyers argued that a continuing debate over the statistical basis used to interpret DNA evidence proves that the procedure does not meet the Frye Standard. Moreover, they argued that the DNA tests, meant to determine whether blood from the murder site and Simpson's car and home matched that of Simpson or the murder victims, were carried out improperly.

DNA profiling is an important contribution to the judicial system in proving innocence and establishing links between a suspect and a particular crime. In an effort to end the uncertainty about the admissibility of DNA evidence in September 1994 President Clinton directed the Federal Bureau of Investigation to set up a national advisory board on DNA quality assurance methods and ordered that federal funds be withheld from labs that did not meet the board's standards.

A genetic fingerprint looks like the bar code which is printed on the labels of goods in a supermarket. It appears in the data presented in court as a set of bars which are separated by particular distances, and that set of bars is a reflection of the DNA sequence which each individual has. Everybody's DNA sequence is different, with the exception of identical twins, who have identical bar codes, though in particular circumstances they could be distinguished too. Bar codes are obtained by taking a DNA sample from a person. Police can start with a very tiny amount of DNA, an unweighable, minuscule amount, and have it amplified to generate bar codes. Provided the chain of evidence is properly established and laboratories which carry out the tests are properly qualified and that due care is taken in processing and analysing the DNA, it is possible to state with virtual certainty that a particular sample came from a particular person. While there is not absolute certainty it is so close to it as to make no difference.

Up to the end of 1993 the Garda forensic unit did not have its own DNA investigation facilities and if the Garda did require DNA profiling it had to be provided outside the jurisdiction. Since the beginning of 1994 the forensic laboratory of the Department of Justice in the Phoenix Park has provided this service. The vast majority of cases involve sexual assault and child abuse – though it is also used in some serious cases of personal injury, murder, burglary and armed robbery. DNA profiling is most useful as a technique in sexual assault cases because the semen deposited in the victim has large quantities of DNA as compared with a blood stain. What is often forgotten is that establishing the identity of an individual from forensic evidence can free an innocent suspect as frequently as securing the conviction of a guilty one.

Unique genetic fingertips can be determined employing DNA from a blood sample or the root of a single hair. Accordingly, a national genetic fingerprint data base would be an invaluable weapon in the fight against crime, since it is virtually impossible for a criminal to avoid leaving hair or skin cells at the scene of the crime. However, this brings problems of its own since innocent passers-by also leave DNA.

Dog buyers have resorted to DNA testing in a bid to expose unscrupulous breeders. The temptation to lie about an animal's pedigree is growing all the time with potential showdogs costing a small fortune. The owners of Crufts champions who are put out to stud can name their price. A number of owners have been duped by breeders who want to make money. One buyer used a DNA test to sue her breeder and won.

In 1983 the wonder racehorse Shergar was abducted from the Ballymany Stud and was never discovered. In the interim there has been extensive speculation about his abduction, with suggestions of links to the IRA, hoax ransom calls and bogus sightings, as well as claims that the horse was killed shortly after an over-ambitious and ill-researched abduction that went tragically wrong. Thirteen years later the exhumation of a carcass in Donegal sparked new hopes of a positive identification of the colt. Were a DNA profile to be built from the carcass and then matched up with the DNA profile from other material – sources of hair and the horse's offspring – it would be possible to achieve an unequivocal identification that the carcass is that of Shergar.

In the beginning
The field of human genetics concentrates on the study of human variability in terms of its causes and effects. The earliest societies to keep records, Babylon, Assyria and Egypt, attributed disabilities to supernatural causes and considered birth abnormalities as signs of good or evil for society itself. These views gradually spread to Greece, Rome and Europe. While the supernatural explanations took precedence, naturalistic explanations for disabilities and for physical similarities and disparities between members of the same family also emerged. Theories on inherited differences can be traced back to the Hippocratic texts and even further in the writings of Anaxagoras (500-428 BC).

Some theories of heredity reflect a seriously flawed understanding of biology but, none the less, were the major source of prescientific guidance on such questions until the Enlightenment. In the light of the work of the pioneering monk

Gregor Mendel, the world has moved from complete genetic innocence to relative genetic experience but there is a long way to go, as geneticists are the first to admit. The new genetics revolution is having an impact on many areas of human activity.

Since the 1980s biotechnology has been changing the face of agriculture.[1] This trend will accelerate in the years ahead as genetic manipulation will create new varieties of basic foods that will have high added value 'quality' traits, which it is hoped will enhance the margins of profitability for food growers, and certainly provide higher quality produce for sale in shops to consumers. Genetic manipulation of plants is based on the transfer of genes that encode desirable traits from one plant variety into another using *in vitro* and *in vivo* methods. This is not an accidental process, but a precise and focused means of introducing genetic variation into plant species. Although there are dire warnings from the doom and gloom merchants about the evils of 'tinkering with nature's creation', genetic manipulation of flora constitutes no more than the acceleration of the process of exploring the extent and possibilities of existing genetic diversity. In the absence of genetic manipulation, this potential would be eventually exploited by natural means by the standard genetic recombination and natural selection events and circumstances where genetically diverse varieties could come into contact.

Researchers at Ohio University have produced a strain of mini-mice, half the normal size, which they say could pave the way to smaller farm animals. The most basic application of genetic knowledge such as changing the direction of natural selection or bringing new mixtures of genes together can do remarkable things. But this will bring new challenges for farmers, some of whom are sceptical about the new methods that have elements of a science fiction plot. The old ways have worked well up to now, so why should they bother with genetic advances? The application of DNA techniques allow for the cloning of gene sequences that code for important characteristics of a plant species such as virus resistance, insecticide resistance and drought tolerance. This requires the identification and isolation of the gene from its natural host, normally another species of the same plant, and multiplying it many times in a specially prepared self-replicating DNA sequence known as plasimid. Plants engineered to contain a gene that confers a useful novel property are termed transgenics.

Since 1983, when the first genetically engineered product – human insulin – reached the market-place, the growth in biotechnological research and development has been explosive and dramatic. This opens up exciting new possibilities of disease control in animals and human beings, of plants resistant to disease and drought, of nitrogen-fixing crops and of dramatically more productive farm animals. Whereas in the past biologists had to rely on mixing thousands of genes by cross-breeding plants or animals and hope for the best, now they can select exactly the genetic trait they want and insert that trait directly into another living organism. In the past historians have spoken of the 'green revolution' to describe the huge increase in the amount of food available world-wide. The genetics revolution will ensure that this trend will accelerate. Already consumers in the developed world are literally tasting the fruits of genetic advances.

The first product to receive regulatory approval in the United States for release onto the market was the Flavr Savr tomato in 1994. This tomato, developed by the US biotechnology firm, Calgene, has had a gene added to it which blocks the production of the pectin-killing enzyme, polygalacturanase (PG). It differs from conventional tomato types in that it has enhanced flavour and an extended shelf-life, taking ten days longer to rot. Other genetically-engineered vegetables which loom on the horizon are a melon with a longer shelf-life, iceberg lettuces in individual serving sizes and celery and carrots genetically engineered to stay crisp for pre-cut snacks.

In June 1997 the European Commission reaffirmed approval for imports of genetically modified maize, overriding import bans by some member states and the objections of the European Parliament. It also approved for the marketing of genetically modified oilseed rape in the EU, which will incorporate labelling. Since 31 July 1997 the Commission has made labelling of new genetically modified crops mandatory. However, while this addresses many of the consumer issues it may not sufficiently address the possible health risks. On 16 July 1997 an EU directive on the legal protection of biotechnological inventions was approved by the European Parliament in Strasbourg.

Environmental groups like Genetic Concern have a number of fears about genetically engineered plants – hence the phrase 'Frankenstein Fodder'. Firstly, there is the fear that such plants, when released, could cross-fertilise their herbicide resistance genes to wild relatives. This would lead to higher weed control costs for farmers but might also lead to an escalated use of herbicides and further destruction of the environment. Secondly, there is concern about the long-term effects of such experiments. Thirdly, there is an anxiety that transgenic vegetables might cause allergic reactions. Against that it might also be possible to genetically engineer food products which do not produce allergic reactions. Finally, it is argued that the new legisaltion on patents will allow multinational companies to tamper with human and animal cells and genes solely in the interests of profit.

The possibilities of new methods of disease control in animals and humankind, for plants resistant to disease and drought, for nitrogen-fixing crops and for dramatically more efficient farm animals now exist. Although, for example, it took over twenty years to develop hybrid seed corn by traditional breeding techniques, genetic engineering allows improvements to be made in years rather than decades. Successful developments in human health-care products and vaccines such as treatment for diabetic, heart attack and cancer patients, encouraged entrepreneurs to develop new products for farmers. Not all such attempts were successful, for example a drug, bovine somatotropin, was developed which was said to offer an increased milk yield of 20 per cent. In the efforts to get the drug on the market as quickly as possible the normal safeguards were not fully observed with the result that the drug was ineffective. The affair was something of a PR disaster for the emerging industry. One of the big challenges of tomorrow's biotechnology is to discover new products which do not have environmental disadvantages.

A new industry
In what Professor David McConnell of Trinity College, Dublin, has described as 'the great theatre of genetic revolution', genes are employed to develop new medical procedures, for example in the design and testing of new drugs and vaccines against AIDS. Now that we know the complete genetic programme of the AIDS virus this information is being used to design and test new drugs and vaccines against the virus. Pharmaceutical companies are investing heavily in new genetically engineered drugs, with sales of 'biotechnology products' reaching $4 billion in 1992 and expected to reach $50 billion by the end of the century. Genes are also being used to develop new medical procedures, with many diabetics being treated with genetically engineered human insulin.

In June 1997 doctors at Addenbrooke's Hospital in Cambridge reported that a pair of obese cousins offer the first evidence that obesity can be attributed to genetic mutation. The cousins have the same mutation in the gene that orders the body to produce leptin, a newly-discovered hormone linked with body fat. Although mice which have been genetically engineered to become obese show genetic mutations, this is the first time a mutated gene has been found in obese humans.

Tay-Sachs disease[2] is a hereditary disease of the central nervous system which crushes the insulating sheath that protects many nerve cells and contributes to a steady loss of movement and premature death. The majority of people with Tay-Sachs are carriers of an identically damaged copy of the gene and descend from a single common ancestor. This gene has been identified and a test for carriers has been developed. Tay-Sachs poses a particular problem for cultures where marriages are arranged between families, such as the Lubavitcher community of Orthodox Jews in New York. Here marriages tend to be the result of the efforts of a matchmaker, who considers the wealth, traditions and health status of the family before attempting to arrange a union. A history of hereditary illness prevents many a marriage. The problem is exacerbated by the fact that in this community, one person in sixteen is a carrier of a single copy of the Tay-Sachs gene, whereas the average in the American population as a whole is one in three hundred. Rabbi Ekstein lost four of his children to Tay-Sachs and, as a consequence of the amount of detailed knowledge about genetics among the community, his siblings found it very difficult to attract marriage partners.

Following the discovery of the Tay-Sachs gene there was initial resistance by some Lubavitch youngsters to being tested. They feared they might be stigmatised and consequently spurned in the 'marriage market'. Rabbi Ekstein came up with a practical solution – although it creates ethical problems of its own in terms of paternalism and the denial of autonomy. His idea was that if people were tested anonymously, and that their parents were told that a particular marriage was undesirable should both of them be carriers, then only a handful of potential marriages, those between two carriers, would be proscribed. Neither person need be told why; the parents would be simply told that the union was undesirable. The union of a carrier and a person free of the Tay-Sachs gene carries no risk of an affected child and thus there can be no impediment to marriage. In this way carriers need never discover their genetic status.

Accordingly, in 1983 Rabbi Ekstein set up Dor Yeshorim, the Association for an Upright Generation. Teenagers are voluntarily tested at school, before they are old enough to contemplate marriage. Each is given a number but the Association does not disclose the results of the test. The number and the recorded status of the child is retained on a computer. When a marriage is planned, a mere telephone call enables the appropriate numbers to be checked against the records. If both partners are found to be carriers, the wedding plans are shelved. As a result the Association is effectively reducing the incidence of Tay-Sachs children born without recourse to abortion.

As it is so isolated from the rest of Europe Finland has its own particular genetic diseases.[3] One is called 'variant late infantile neuronal ceroid lipofuscosis' or vLINCL, which is concentrated near the town of Lapua. The consequences of the disease are very distressing. Affected children appear clumsy in their first few years, and with the passage of time they suffer from seizures, go blind and become paralysed. Normally, they die in early adulthood. It is a recessive gene, so two copies of the gene, one from both parents, are required to produce the condition. Twenty-one patients from eighteen families have been identified; in practically all of the cases there was no known history of the condition in the family. Church records established that twenty-four of the thirty-six parents of the affected children were, without their knowing it, related, sometimes in a number of different ways. The oldest known ancestor lived in the village of Kauhajoki at the beginning of the seventeenth century – thirteen generations before his affected descendants of today were born. On this basis we can conclude that for almost four centuries the gene passed through healthy people who carried only a single copy and were unaware of its existence. Eventually, though, two streams of DNA converged in a sick child, showing that these parents were indeed related. This example illustrates the way in which family trees can branch from a distant individual to meet again in people alive today.

The footprints of history

Genetics can also unlock many of the mysteries of the past. It has taught us that both Margaret Thatcher and John Major descend from John and Elizabeth Crust, who farmed in Leake, in Lincolnshire, in the eighteenth century; making them fifth cousins, once removed.[4] Prince Charles can trace his descent from Edward III along some three thousand different lines; but Princess Diana had four thousand lines from the same person.

Archaeologists, anthropologists, linguists and historians are using genetics in an exciting way. Modern DNA sequence data, analysed using the 'molecular clock', have revealed that human beings separated from the chimpanzees about six million years ago and sensationally suggests that all humankind is descended from one mother who lived in Africa about 200,000 years ago. One goal which has emerged in recent times is a family tree of all human societies using a massive survey of genes and languages.

Genetics has done two things in terms of Darwin's theory of evolution. Darwin did not know how characteristics were inherited: he knew they were but not how they were and he was very confused about that. In the 1920s a group of eminent geneticists established that evolution could be explained in terms of genes. That was before we knew that genes were made of DNA. The dramatic new contribution of genetics to the theory of evolution is that it has allowed us to measure the time at which any two organisms had a common ancestor. This is established through the science of molecular evolution, which derives from genetics and allows us to compare the DNA of any two species, for example when we compare the DNA sequence of a human being with that of a chimpanzee we find that they are 98.4 per cent identical. We had a common ancestor with the chimpanzee somewhere between three and five million years ago but we are not descendants of the chimpanzee. If we were to compare the DNA sequence of a human being with a gorilla there would be more differences. If we went on to the DNA of the horse we would see that our DNA is much different from that of horses but we are still obviously related. The general rule is that the more similar the organism the more similar the DNA.

Genetics may provide the key which unlocks the secrets of the past and provides many answers for anthropologists and archaeologists, and is likely to have the same impact on archaeology as carbon dating. It is said, for example, that 25 per cent of the genes of the Australian population are Irish, and we can now establish what percentage of the Australian population's genes are Irish. At the moment groups of scientists are coming together and co-operating worldwide in their gene analysis of different peoples in the Human Gene Diversity Project.

The genetics of skin pigment determine that many Irish people have pale skins and consequently Ireland has the third highest incidence of skin cancer in the world after Australia and South Africa. On the other hand it has been suggested that black skin is more prone to frost bite than white. During the savage winter of 1917 a French doctor working in the trenches recorded more than a thousand cases of 'frozen foot' in Senegalese troops but none in whites.

New genetic knowledge will also shed light on some of the greatest mysteries of our time. The interaction of nature and nurture has been an enduring source of fascination but the discovery of DNA has raised this interest to a new plain. When the function of each gene is identified, inheritance is established. The effect of our environment on individual development will follow. Families with a hereditary illness can reduce the risk of passing it on if the method of inheritance is ascertained.

Biological science has arrived at a good working knowledge of how the major organs in the body, apart from the brain, function. In recent times they have been striving to remedy this situation, in particular in relation to consciousness, the process whereby we are aware of our own existence and of the existence of the world. However, others argue that the tools of science are unable to comprehend such a rich mystery. The main player in the consciousness debate is Francis Crick. In 1953 Crick emerged onto the centre stage when he, with James Watson, worked out the structure of DNA, which explained the chemical basis of genetic inheritance. Afterwards Crick moved into the realm of neuroscience and the culmination of his research was published with a flourish in 1994 in *The Astonishing Hypothesis*. So what is so astonishing?

> Your joys and your sorrows, your memories and your ambitions, your sense of personal identity and free will, are in fact no more than the behaviour of a vast assembly of nerve cells and their associated molecules.[6]

Some of the claims for genetic knowledge are more speculative. The Earl of Chesterfield cast a succinct cold eye on sex in the eighteenth century when he remarked: 'The pleasure is momentary, the position ridiculous and the expense damnable.' However, it has been argued that sex is a worthy occupation because it achieves genetic hygiene. R. E. Michod, in *Eros and Evolution: A Natural Philosophy of Sex,* suggests that sex evolved because it is such an effective mechanism for repairing damaged genetic material, thereby guaranteeing the pristine quality of the germ cells that unite to form a new and unique person.

The research biologist Dr Robin Baker, in his *Sperm Wars – Infidelity, Sexual Conflict And Other Bedroom Conflicts,*[7] argues that genes are the reason why people in the middle of a stable, satisfying relationship get the urge to be unfaithful. He claims that it is because our bodies are programmed to shop around for genes.

Genomics

For some time now we have been aware of the fact that many diseases are the product of a complex interaction between genes, behaviour and environment, but the exact interrelationship has been shrouded in mystery. In the immediate future, scientists will end much of this uncertainty, and many areas of clinical practice could change radically as a result. It is hoped that this will result in earlier and more accurate prediction and diagnosis of many major disorder and new opportunities for prevention and treatment. The science underlying this is known as genomics, which is the study of genetic control of body functions, both in health and disease.

There are approximately five thousand different genetic diseases and roughly one child in fifty is born with a significant genetic disorder. Asthma, allergies, diabetes, vascular disease, cancer and many other diseases are caused by a combination of genetic and environmental factors. Approximately a hundred genes have been identified which are related to cancer, including some which have been associated with breast cancer. At the moment we can prevent many genetic diseases such as cystic fibrosis, muscular dystrophy, haemophilia and, in some cases, advise about the risk of cancers.

The ability to identify genes and their functions opens up a genetic Pandora's Box; where a disease is caused by a disorder in one particular gene, it means health care professionals can diagnose that disease not by looking for the symptoms but by identifying the gene and its disorder. Moreover, the disease could be identified before it manifests itself, or even before the person with that disease has been born. Since genes determine the manufacture of proteins and effectively constitute the building-blocks of the human body, our ability to identify genes may also affect our ability to build that human body. If we could alter a particular gene, either in terms of content or function, we might be able to prevent, for example, the growth of cancerous cells.

Genes are functional segments of DNA, the molecule in

chromosomes that specifies the composition of the various proteins that occur in organisms. Genes or, more precisely, specific functional segments of DNA, can decisively influence whether and at what rate a particular protein, as well as the proteins specified by other proximate genes, are synthesised. Human DNA is made up of two ribbons consisting of alternating sugar and phosphate molecules wound into a double helix. These ribbons are linked by rungs which are moulded by two bases, one attached to each ribbon. There are four kinds of bases in DNA: adenine (A), thymine (T), cytosine (C) and guanine (G). On any strand of the double helix, the four kinds of bases can occur in any sequence, but their shapes are such that, in order to fit together into rungs, every A on the one strand must lie opposite a T on the other strand, and every C must lie opposite a G (Fig. 1).

Figure 1: DNA Double Helix

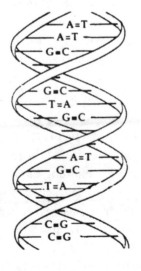

Each gene is responsible for producing a single, unique protein. There are approximately 100,000 genes in each cell. The complete set of genetic information about an organism is known as the genome. In humans, the thousand of genes are grouped together into forty-six chromosomes arranged in twenty-three pairs. The twenty-three pairs of chromosomes are contained in DNA, the material which stores genetic information in each cell.

These genes are arranged on each chromosome in linear sequence, for example the gene which determines an individual's eye-colour has its own place on a particular chromosome. A different allele (the name given to one of a number of alternative forms of gene) at that particular place may produce a different eye-colour. Sometimes two corresponding genes may be identical, for example both alleles would produce brown eyes. However, they may be different, for example one gene for green, one for blue. A gene is termed dominant if it is always expressed even when paired with a gene for a different trait, thus brown eyes are a dominant trait while blue eyes are recessive.

The human reproductive cells, eggs or sperm, contain only one set of chromosomes and therefore only one copy of each gene. As the egg is fertilised, these so-called germ cells combine to generate a new set of forty-six chromosomes bearing pairs of genes. Following fertilisation cells multiply by splitting into halves. As each cell divides, the DNA in that cell is duplicated. Each person's cell should contain an exact replica of the DNA in each fertilised egg from which the person has grown. However, during the process of division and duplication, a mutation occurs when the link in the DNA chain may be altered. In many cases these mutations constitute no threat and could even be beneficial, but sometimes, for example in the case of cancerous growths, they are harmful.

2

GENESIS REVISITED[1]

It is the best of times. It might be the worst of times. Were
Charles Dickens alive today he might describe the genetics
revolution this way. Since the cloning of Dolly the sheep on 23
February 1997, the doom and gloom merchants have had a field
day. The ghost of Frankenstein has been regularly invoked and
terms like 'the slippery slope' have been thrown around. Too often
hysteria and ignorance have taken the place of measured analysis.
The details of some of the proposed experiments would fit
comfortably in Aldous Huxley's *Brave New World* or George
Orwell's *1984*.

Dolly, named after singer Dolly Parton, was cloned with tissue
taken from the udder of a six-year-old sheep, then cultured in a
laboratory. A nucleus from one cell was transferred to an egg which
had its nucleus, or genetic material, removed. The egg was then
implanted into a third sheep where it developed normally and led
to the birth of Dolly who is genetically identical to the sheep from
which her cells were removed.

Significantly, President Clinton responded immediately to the
news of Dolly by requesting the National Bioethics Advisory

Commission to review what were termed these 'troubling' implications. His action highlighted the lack of government control in this sensitive area of research. A loophole existed because of the failure to provide legislation authorising federal funding for human embryo research, thus leaving the field open to unregulated private institutions.

The variety in the comments of the Commission give grounds both for encouragement and concern. On the one hand Thomas Murray, Director of the Centre for Biomedical Ethics at Case Western Reserve University, claimed that cloning 'really goes to the heart of what's significant about having children, being a parent, the interweaving of generations and ... whether it is elevating narcissism to new heights.' However, another Commission member, Dr Masood Khatamee, produced the ethically flawed argument that 'if we stop it in this country, other parts of the world will be ahead of us'.

Leading British physicist and Nobel laureate Joseph Rotblat fuelled a major ethical debate with his warning that the technology which created Dolly constituted a threat to humankind's future. For years he has campaigned against nuclear weapons but in the wake of Dolly claimed that scientific advances could determine the whole fate of humankind. His concern was that genetic engineering would result in other means of mass destruction becoming even more readily available than nuclear weapons.

However, Dr Ian Wilmut of the Roslin Institute in Edinburgh, the pioneering scientist responsible for Dolly, countered by pointing out the potential of the technology to create animals that can produce lifesaving human blood products and to study genetic disorders that can provide agents to fight diseases. The discovery would enable scientists to get closer than ever to finding a cure for human and animal diseases such as cancer, cystic fibrosis, emphysema, BSE and CJD. The pharmaceutical industry is also likely to profit as genetically-identical living organisms can be developed which will enable the production of new and more beneficial drugs. New fuel was added to the ethical debate when another sheep clone, Polly, was born on 9 July 1997, but this time a human gene had been included in her genetic makeup.

Given the expense it does not make economic sense to reproduce animals using this complicated technology when conventional breeding achieves the same result for free. An exception might be the case of elite animals like champion racehorses such as Danoli. Inevitably, though, the cloning of Dolly and Polly led to the question: If a sheep can be cloned, can human cloning be far behind? The fingerprints of history dictate that many people will be concerned with this prospect.

The genetic skeletons in the closet

The great Victorian writer Thomas Henry Huxley (known as Darwin's bulldog because of his vigorous defence of his idol) observed: 'It is the customary fate of new truths to begin as heresies and to end as superstitions.'[2] His remarks were prompted by the reaction to Darwin's *The Origin of Species* which was first published in 1859. The book created a tidal wave of sensationalism principally because it seemed to remove the necessity for a direct link between God and humankind. The wife of the Bishop of Worcester waded into the controversy with a telling remark to a family friend: 'My dear, let us hope that it is not true – but, if it is, let us pray that it does not become generally known!'

The subtext of Darwin's evolutionary theory was natural selection – what would subsequently be known as 'the survival of the fittest', although it was Herbert Spencer and not Darwin who coined the phrase. In a clever adaptation of a more famous aphorism, Oscar Wilde put the idea succinctly: 'Nothing succeeds like excess.'

The most famous line in *The Origin of Species* expresses the hope that 'light may be shed on man and his origins'. Darwin compared humans with monkeys and apes to establish their common ancestry. He claimed: 'Man still bears in his bodily frame the indelible stamp of his lowly origin.' W. S. Gilbert expressed it cleverly: 'Darwinian man, though well-behaved, is really just a monkey shaved.'[3]

Darwin's ideas would also find an airing in the world of fiction. As most English readers know, in Edgar Rice Burrough's classic novel *Tarzan of the Apes* the great swinger was proved to be the son of Lord Greystoke by virtue of the inky fingermarks in a childhood notebook.

One of the less inspired sections of *The Origin of Species* was the idea of inheritance by the mixing of bloods. This idea lingered for over a century and was particularly influential in racehorse breeding. A mare who had borne a foal by mating with a non-stud stallion was struck off as her blood was deemed to be polluted and incapable of bearing a pure-bred horse. More surprisingly, a survey of elderly women in Bristol in 1973 showed that 50 per cent of them believed that there was a chance of a woman having a black baby if she had had conjugal relations with a black man even many years before. However, the mixing of blood myth was easily shot down by means of a simple experiment. The blood from a black rabbit was transfused to a white one to see if the latter would have black offspring. It did not. Darwin did not know it at the time but somebody else had already found the answers to many of the questions that troubled him so much.

All peas great and small
European doctors in the seventeenth and eighteenth centuries passionately discussed the 'performatist' theory in terms of whether or not the whole organism was formed in the ovum or sperm. However, the lack of empirical evidence caused the debate to perish. The situation was transformed with the publication of the results of Gregor Mendel's experiments in 1865. The Austrian, an

Augustinian monk and botanist of sorts (he started a science degree but never finished it), experimented with crossing varieties of the pea in terms of colour and shape of seed. Mendel went on to count all types of and combinations in the offspring for several generations. On the basis of these experiments he formulated the scientific laws that shaped the foundations of modern genetics and provided the correct biological theory for the similarities and dissimilarities between offspring, namely, that the germ cells (sperm and ova) are the unchanging forms in the dynamics of inheritance. He was the first to establish that offspring are not the average of their parents and that inheritance is based on differences rather than similarities.

It is a striking comment on the cultural isolation of prominent scientists at the time that Darwin was totally ignorant of Mendel's work, despite publishing during the same period. Mendel's concept of the gene would have provided answers to many of Darwin's major questions, especially as to the mode of inheritance of specific characteristics. More surprisingly, Mendel's work remained unused by scientists and was eventually rediscovered only in 1900.

Mendel's findings were rapidly found to apply to hundreds of characteristics in both animals and plants and slowly led to clear and less controversial applications in medical genetics, and to evidence that genes were composed of the content of DNA molecules, the building-blocks of protein synthesis common to life in all its forms. Techniques in molecular biology progressively laid the groundwork of our contemporary understanding of gene action. Molecular biologists regularly recombine particles of DNA to produce new life forms in bacteria, plants and chemicals. Mendel's laws were also shown to apply to humans as much as any other creatures and used to explain all manner of patterns of family resemblance. In the wake of the advances of Mendelian genetics, doctors and other scientists applied genetic knowledge to problems of inherited disorders.

It is noteworthy that are many parallels between theories of economics and of evolution, for example Darwin was greatly influenced by the pioneering work of Thomas Malthus who was deeply distressed by the new slums of the English cities of the eighteenth century. In his Essay on the Principles of Population Malthus claimed that population will inevitably outstrip resources. Darwin admitted that it was reading this that first gave him the idea of natural selection. Three years after the publication of *The Origin of the Species* Marx wrote to Friedrich Engels that: 'it is remarkable how Darwin recognises among beasts and plants his English society, with its division of labour, competition, opening up of new markets, inventions, and the Malthusian struggle for existence.'

Perhaps Darwin's greatest legacy is his insight that nothing makes sense in biology except in the context of evolution. Darwin's vast intellectual explorations were to a large extent prompted by his conviction that there is a moral imperative to do everything possible to build a better future for subsequent generations. His convictions were shared by his cousin Francis Galton.

Galton was a fascinating character. Born into a family of wealthy, Quaker gunmakers he has the distinction of having published the first weather map but, more curiously, he also produced the first beauty map of Britain, based on his secret grading of the local women on a scale of one to five. The women from Aberdeen had cause to wonder – they were at the bottom of the list! He discovered that chimpanzees have fingerprints and illustrated this by pasting the appropriate impression near that made by the prime minister of the time, Gladstone. The titles of his three hundred scientific papers indicate the breadth of his interests. They include: *Three generations of lunatic cats; Visions for sane persons; Cutting a round cake on scientific principles; The relative sensitivity of men and women at the nape of the neck; Pedigree moths; The average flush of excitement; On spectacles for divers; Statistical inquiries into the efficacy of prayer; Strawberry cure for gout; Good and bad temper in English families; Nuts and men;* and the *pièce de résistance, Arithmetic by smell.*

Relative success

Galton could be considered the grandfather of the current interest in genetics. He founded the first human genetics institute in the world in London and introduced the notion that human attributes are coded into the unique inheritance which everyone receives from their ancestors. His particular interest was in the inheritance of genius. No doubt the fact that he considered himself to belong to this category fuelled his interest in this topic. In his book *Hereditary Genius,* published in 1869, he explored the ancestry of various high achievers and proved, to his own satisfaction at least, that ability was inborn and not acquired.

Galton favoured active interference with human evolution. Not alone did he back the idea of breeding from the best but he believed in sterilising those whose inheritance did not meet with his approval. If economies could be planned, then so could genes. The concern for the rights of the unborn was matched by a callous indifference to the rights of many of the living.

In 1883 Galton coined the term 'eugenics' (from the Greek, meaning 'wellborn') to describe a new 'science' that would focus upon improving the human race by judicious matching of parents possessing 'superior' traits. Its main purpose was, in his own words, 'to check the birth rate of the Unfit and improve the race by furthering the productivity of the fit by early marriages of the best stock'. In so doing he dispatched the new field of genetics into a cul-de-sac.

This was not a totally novel idea. Since the time of Plato, if not earlier, philosophers have consistently urged vibrant, healthy, creative and intelligent people to reproduce. The other side of the coin was that people who were deemed to be incapable of playing a productive role in society were discouraged with equal frequency both by tradition and, in extreme cases, by legislation, from bearing children. Although the impetus for both a positive eugenics (promoting childbearing among the most 'fit') and a negative eugenics (dissuading parenthood among the 'unfit') is steeped in history, it was only in the latter part of the nineteenth century that the notion of selective breeding based on systematic, ostensible scientific principles was seriously advocated.

Plato's Utopia contained eugenic principles for selection of spouses for reproduction. It has been argued, not very convincingly, that part of the Mosaic Code (Lev 18:6-13) prohibiting incest was in part related to eugenic concern, due to an insight into the recurrence of birth defects from sexual relations between close relatives. While no biblical text specifically deals with prevention of birth defects through marital laws, incest is clearly seen as ethically unacceptable. A more credible source for the first ethical reflection on eugenics in any social or religious system is the Talmud. This collection of rabbinic writings dating from AD 400, rules that a man may not marry into a family afflicted with epilepsy, leprosy, or a similar disease.

In medieval Japan, the science of dactylomancy, judging personality from fingerprints, contended that people with complex patterns would probably be good craftsmen, those with many loops lacked perseverance, and those whose fingers carried an arched pattern were both merciless and crude. Early eugenic theories betrayed this type of prejudice and wild speculation.

Galton's supporters developed his premise that certain behavioural patterns or characteristics of personality could be identified in people and passed on through a programme of selective mating. They went on to argue that many negative traits could be traced to a hereditary legacy, so that criminals, paupers, alcoholics, prostitutes, and others with undesirable propensities had reached their state in life simply as a result of their genetic inheritance.

This view was also championed by George Bernard Shaw, who

often appeared on platforms with Galton. Shaw observed initially with a hint of humour: 'Men and women select their wives and husbands far less carefully than they select their cashiers and cooks.' Later a much more sinister note crept in: 'Extermination must be put on a humane basis if it is ever to be carried out humanely and apologetically as well as thoroughly.'

In *Back to Methuselah* Shaw wrote that 'if we desire a certain type of civilization we must exterminate the sort of people who do not fit into it'. In a scientific vision of the world to come, *Anticipations of the Reaction of Scientific Progress upon Human Life and Thought* (1901), H. G. Wells wrote in favour of euthanasia for 'the weak and sensual' and genocide for 'the dingy white and yellow people who do not come into the needs of efficiency'.

Galton bequeathed £45,000 to found the Laboratory of National Eugenics (shortly afterwards, in an early example of political correctness, its name was changed to the Galton Laboratory as eugenical ideas went out of a fashion) at University College London. Galton's wealthy followers claimed that their purpose was to ensure the 'survival of the fittest'. If economies could be planned, then so could genes. Galton even went so far as to argue: 'There are no people, there are only genes.'

The survival of the richest

Galton's views, like Darwin's, were eagerly embraced by many of his contemporaries from right across the ideological spectrum though, crucially, from the upper echelons of socio-economic life. A notable disciple was Herbert Spencer, the founder of 'Social Darwinism', the belief that poverty and wealth are inevitable because they represent the biological rules which govern society. It was he who coined the phrases 'survival of the fittest' and 'evolution'. In fact, it might be argued that the hidden agenda of this movement was the survival of the richest.

Spencer exerted a major influence on the intelligentsia of the time and used *The Origin of Species* as a rationale for the excesses of nineteenth-century capitalism. The idea that evolution excused injustice was a popular one among the wealthy elite. After his death *The Times* wrote: 'England has lost the most widely celebrated and influential of her sons.'

In 1910 a political leader expressed sentiments similar to Galton's. When he was Home Secretary Winston Churchill stated: 'The unnatural and increasingly rapid growth of the feeble-minded and insane classes, coupled as it is with steady restriction among all the thrifty, energetic and superior stocks constitutes a national and race danger which is impossible to exaggerate. I feel that the source from which the stream of madness is fed should be cut off and sealed off before another year has passed.' Churchill's comments were regarded as so inflammatory by subsequent British governments that they were not made public until 1992.

This school of thought proved to be more popular in America than in the UK. A Eugenics Record Office (now Cold Spring Harbor Laboratory) was established on Long Island Sound, employing two hundred field workers who were dispatched to collect pedigrees. Their 750,000 genetic records ranged from studies of inherited disease and colour blindness, to recording the inheritance of shyness and moral control. Medical practitioners began to question whether their duty to future patients outweighed their responsibilities to current patients. Twenty-five thousand people were sterilised lest they pass on feeble-mindedness or criminality to future generations. One judge even went so far as to compare sterilisation with vaccination, claiming that the common good overrode individual rights and that 'three generations of imbeciles were enough'.[4]

The eugenical message was often promoted under the guise of financial rectitude. In 1926, at the Sesquicentennial Exhibition in Philadelphia, the American Eugenics Society had a board with flashing lights counting the $100 per second allegedly spent on people with 'bad heredity'. In the 1990s one of the proponents of the Human Genome Project suggested that the enterprise would be self-financing by 'curing' the problem of schizophrenia by terminating the pregnancies of women shown to be carrying the undiscovered gene for the disease. Is this a warning that in our own time genetics could be used as an excuse to discriminate against those with disabilities in order to save money?

Genetic exploration is still valiantly striving to overcome its discredited history. In the past eugenics attracted people who were trying to promote a particular agenda, for example those who argued that it was possible to improve the human race by 'selective breeding' or by the elimination of 'inferior specimens'. Things came to a head with the monstrous barbarism of the Nazis.

The ethical fragrance that marks aspects of Darwin's and Galton's theories was less to the forefront in their attitudes to people who did not meet up to their exacting standards. It is no accident that Hitler's autobiography, *Mein Kampf,* has as its title part of a Darwinian phrase, the 'struggle' for existence. During his time in prison Hitler read the classic German text on human genetics, *The Principles of Human Heredity and Race Hygiene,* by the director of the Berlin Institute for Anthropology, Human Heredity and Eugenics, Eugene Fischer. Fischer wrote: 'The question of the quality of our hereditary endowment is a hundred times more important than the dispute over capitalism or socialism.' Many of Fischer's ideas are echoed in *Mein Kampf:* 'Whoever is not bodily and spiritually healthy and worthy shall not have the right to pass on his suffering in the body of his children.'

Galton's theories had found another sympathetic ear in Germany in the person of embroyologist Ernst Haeckel. His reading of *The Origin of Species* helped him to conclude that every animal relived its evolutionary past during its embryonic development. More importantly, it led him to establish the Monist League, which attracted thousands of members in Germany before the First World War. Its principal concern was to nurture those of the finest biological pedigree at the expense of others. Haeckel went so far as to suggest that 'the whole history of nations can be explained by means of natural selection' and that 'social rules are the natural laws of heredity and adaptation'. He went on to argue that the evolutionary destiny of the Germans was to overcome inferior peoples: 'The Germans have deviated furthest from the common form of ape-like men ... The lower races are psychologically nearer to the animals than to civilized Europeans. We must, therefore, assign a totally different value to their lives.'

In power Hitler took this premise to its natural conclusion by destroying the people he saw as less favoured and attempting to breed from the best. Four hundred thousand sterilisations were performed on those considered unworthy to pass on their genes, sometimes by the covert use of X-rays as the victims were filling in forms.

A symptom of the prejudice of the time was that on foot of a road accident a Nazi party member received a blood transfusion from a Jew after he had been in a road accident. He was hauled before a disciplinary court to see if he should be excluded from the Party. When it emerged that the donor had fought in the First World War it was grudgingly conceded that his blood might be up to the required standard. Interestingly, the German eugenics movement was totally opposed to abortion, though naturally they made exceptions for the biologically unfit, and imposed stiff penalties on any doctor willing to comply with a request for an abortion.

In 1933 Hitler promulgated the Eugenic Sterilisation Law. It is worth noting in passing that by 1931, thirty US states also had compulsory sterilisation laws, which applied to a wide variety of 'hereditary defectives'. By 1936 the German Society for Race Hygiene had over sixty branches, while doctorates in racial science were offered at several German universities. It is a disturbing fact that half of those at the Wannsee Conference, which decided on the final solution of the Jewish problem, had doctorates, chiefly in anthropology. By and large they defended their crimes on scientific grounds. In this climate the prevailing view was that certain people were inferior because of their inheritance. The legacy of this thought lingers with us in a very tangible way today.

Elisabeth's list

Hitler wept openly at Elisabeth Nietzsche's funeral in 1935. Although she was constantly overshadowed by her more famous brother, Friedrich, in a very real sense her vision has outlived his.

In Paraguay there is a remote village with a peculiar name: Nueva Germania, or New Germany. Its people look remarkably different from their neighbours. The majority have blonde hair and blue eyes. Their names are Germanic rather than Spanish. These people are the descendants of an unusual experiment; an attempt to improve humankind. Their ancestors were chosen from the people of Saxony in 1886 by Elisabeth Nietzsche.

Her brother Friedrich, the famous philosopher, had uttered the chilling phrase: 'What in the world has caused more damage than the follies of the compassionate?' Yet it was Elisabeth who was entrusted with the task of selecting splendid specimens on the basis of the purity of their blood. The aim was to found a community so favoured in its genetic endowment that it would be the seed of a new race of supermen (and, presumably, superwomen, though feminist sensitives were not a priority at the time). The idea had initially been floated by the composer Richard Wagner who planned to visit the community but never got around to it. Today the people of Nueva Germania are poor, inbred and disease-ridden.

A major flaw in these purportedly 'scientific' studies was that they virtually ignored the effects of environment on human achievement. Scant attention was given to the difficulty of analysing a particular character trait such as intelligence that is shaped by a multiplicity of factors like education, family influence and heredity. By the mid-1940s increased sophistication in the study of genetics had shattered many of the myths of eugenic theory that had arisen in the early part of the century. The fall of Nazi Germany, the state that most actively promoted the doctrine of eugenical theory, was perhaps the final nail in the eugenics coffin.

In our own time the most distasteful arguments of classical eugenics are held in general disrepute, for example that people with disabilities should be strictly prohibited from marrying or that some races or ethnic groups are genetically inferior to others but, although the term 'eugenics' itself is seldom heard, the notion that society should have some say in regulating reproduction remains in vogue.

The major ethical difficulty with this position is that it gives precedence to the obligation to nurture humankind's genes at the expense of those who bear them. Since the Second World War geneticists have become more aware of the limits of their science and have forsaken the quest to establish a super race. However, there are still echoes of this thinking to be found. In 1988 the *Chinese People's Daily* reported a scheme to ban the marriage of those with mental disease unless they were sterilised, with a chilling claim: 'Idiots give birth to idiots.' Recent events in Singapore give further grounds for concern about the new eugenics. In Singapore the state actively promotes reproduction among the educated and prevents it in the poor and uneducated in the hope of creating a super-intelligent gene pool.

In this century, application of this eugenical philosophy led to such morally unacceptable practices as the large-scale sexual sterilisation of epileptics, the mentally ill and the retarded, restrictions on the immigration of some ethnic groups, and prohibition of marriages between people of differing racial backgrounds. These practices were justified on the basis of supposedly 'scientific' criteria based on eugenical studies which argued that parents with disabilities always produced 'unfit' children and that the people of some nations and ethnic groups were genetically inferior to people of other nations; and that mixing the genes of superior and inferior races would dilute the total gene pool to the detriment of humanity.

Gender-selection is another form of eugenics which reproductive technology facilitates. It is our chromosomes which determine our sex. Women have two 'X' chromosomes, men a single 'X' chromosome and a much smaller 'Y' chromosome. Consequently while all eggs have an X, sperm are of two kinds, X or Y. At fertilisation, both XY males and XX females are created in equal quantity. Some years ago the Indian government shut down clinics which chose the gender of a baby by examining the chromosomes of the foetus and aborting those with two Xs. Over two thousand prenancies were terminated per annum on this basis in Bombay. The procedure was considered necessary because of the large dowries which had to be provided when daughters were married off. The clinics advertised with slogans which struck a chord with many people: 'Spend six hundred rupees now, save fifty thousand later.' It is important to stress that practices such as routine amniocentesis followed by abortion of female foetuses in India is a social rather than technological problem. There are several ways to make an effective choice of sex, notably IVF. This procedure of course raises ethical issues of its own.

Genetics shatters Plato's myth of the absolute, that there exists one ideal form of human being from which there are rare deviations such as those who have an inborn disease. However, genetic research holds out new possibilities for reinforcing social control – and, more sinisterly, for legitimising that control. A 1972 survey of American obstetricians found that 'although only 6 per cent favoured sterilization for their private patients, 14 per cent favoured it for the welfare patients. For welfare mothers who had borne illegitimate children, 97 per cent ... favoured sterilization.'[5]

This is classic eugenic philosophy. However, eugenics raises its ugly head in more subtle forms, for example testing prospective patients to establish if they are carriers of genetic 'defects' could lead to many people being labelled 'defective'. Not only those who manifest the condition but the carriers also may viewed as falling short of 'perfection'. Such tests are ostensibly about increasing people's choices, but we need to be alert to the possibility of an ideological subtext. In this context the words of Bentley Glass, retiring as President of the American Association for the Advancement of Science in 1971, make for sober reading:

> In a world where each pair must limited, on the average, to two offspring and no more, the right that must become paramount is the right of every child to be born with a social, physical and mental constitution based on a sound genotype. No parent will in that future time have the right to burden society with a malformed or mentally incompetent child.[6]

3
AFTER THE BRAVE NEW WORLD

Steven Spielberg's hugely successful film *Jurassic Park* brought the world of DNA, albeit in a fanciful way, to a mass audience. In 1988 an international research organisation, the Human Genome Project, was established to co-ordinate the work being done by genetic scientists. It has been termed 'biology's answer to the Apollo Space Programme' and is a massive project. Hundreds, if not thousands, of top scientists particularly in the US but also in Europe and Japan, are trying to locate and analyse the 100,000 (approximately) genes that make up our genetic inheritance, a task likely to be completed in the early years of the next century, at an estimated cost of three billion dollars.

In the European initiative, the focus is on identifying and characterising genes of importance to the development of disease, while the American and Japanese programmes are committed to mapping the entire genome, i.e. the combination of genes acquired from one's biological parents. When this process is complete humankind will have a picture of what the 'average' person is like at the molecular level what has been described in a recent, though curiously anachronistically titled book by Walter Bodmer and

Robin McKie as 'the book of man'.[1] The 'book' they talk about refers to the message written in the DNA strands in every cell of the body of every human being. It is a message which contains the instructions for constructing and maintaining a human being as a living organism.

Put more simply the project is an attempt to discover which genes are responsible for which features of our physical make-up, for example the exact genetic characteristics which cause one person to be right-handed and another left-handed. The goal is to produce a map of the twenty-three human chromosomes pinpointing the location of each gene, and the sequences, in DNA's four-letter code. As the individual genes are mapped, this also increases the possibilities of detecting disposition to disease by diagnosing and pinpointing genetic carriers, including the detection of disposition to diseases which may not develop until a much later stage.

The genetic Promised Land

Andrea Bonnicksen uses a striking image to describe this development. She details the scene on the top floor of the Gold Museum in Bogota, Colombia, where visitors are ushered into a dark, windowless room and heavy doors are closed behind them. They stand in the darkness until, slowly, like a 'ringed and rising sun', lights come on around them and they discover they are surrounded by 'glimmering, lustrous' gold in an awesome display of wealth and beauty. She argues that we are at an analogous state in genetics, when the lights come up and we marvel at the richness of the discoveries in DNA analysis.[2]

The Human Genome Project is a concerted effort to map and determine the base sequences of all the functional DNA sequences within 'the' human genome. The study is not just for molecular biologists – the scientists who study the structure and function of genes and DNA. The maps of the human chromosome that will be drawn up will be important to each of us. Who will be entitled to know what about whose genes? How do we best cultivate the fruits of science in an ethically responsible way? The inevitable debate that will be generated may lead to a greater level of 'DNA literacy', i.e. what everyone should know in order to arrive at an informed view of 'the genetic agenda'.

As Steve Jones points out: 'Genetics is the key to the past. Every gene must have an ancestor. This means that patterns of inherited variation can be used to piece together a picture of history more complete than from any other source. Each gene is a message from our forebears and together they contain the whole story of human evolution. Everyone is a living fossil, carrying within themselves a record which goes back to the beginnings of humanity and far beyond.'[3]

Genetics can help us to understand puzzling phenomena like the unique inheritance of the Pennsylvania Amish. Almost a hundred babies in this community have been born with six fingers and restricted growth, a condition almost unknown elsewhere. Each child is descended from Samuel King, a founder of the community.

Genetic information can also throw new light on old problems, as, for example the discovery of 'genomic imprinting', whereby the effects of a particular gene sometimes seem to depend on whether it is passed on by mother or by a father. The effects of imprinting are evident in the inheritance of Huntington's Disease. The age at which the symptoms of nerve damage first appear varies from individual to individual. People who inherit the gene from their father show its effects sooner than do those receiving a copy of the same type of gene from the mother. Children of affected men normally show the first symptoms at an average age of thirty-three while children of affected women tend to have an additional nine years before the condition takes its toll. Genes are also being used to develop new medical procedures; we now know the complete genetic programme of the HIV virus and this knowledge is being used to design and test new drugs and vaccines against AIDS.

It is significant that Steve Jones called his award-winning book *The Language of Genes* because of the parallels between biological evolution and the evolution of language. His argument is that genetics, like language, is a set of inherited instructions passed from generation to generation. Genes are a vocabulary, a grammar (the way in which the information is collated and structured), and a literature, the thousands of instructions required to make a human being. Genes, like language, evolve. Accordingly, our primary task is to learn to read the language of genes. Hence the Human Genome Project.

There are clear commercial benefits in this study which is evident in the scramble to patent the products of genes as they are discovered. The patents may be licences to print money for those who discover treatments, even tests, for genetic disease.

Some of its advocates have compared the Human Genome Project to the biblical injunction 'know thyself'. Others see it as a scientific equivalent to the search for the Holy Grail. It has also been described as 'the most astonishing adventure of our time' and 'today's most important scientific undertaking'. Sir Walter Bodmer describes it as 'one of mankind's greatest odysseys'. Supporters suggest that the project promises to reveal 'what it is to be human' and to 'illuminate the determinants of human disease ... that are the root of many current societal problems'.[4]

A lot of (genetic) knowledge is a dangerous thing

Steve Jones acknowledges that the ethical problems which arise from interfering with DNA are more subtle than those which arise in most other moral questions.[5] Nowhere might the old adage 'a little knowledge is a dangerous thing' apply more directly than in genetics, which can tell us things we may not want to hear. As this process accelerates the probable date of our death might become available to us. How many of us would want this information?

The consequences of this new information open the ethical equivalent of a Pandora's Box. The difficult questions require urgent attention and cannot be left to the leisurely time-frame suggested by Bodmer and McKie because the answers are needed now. Indeed there is much excited talk today about 'the final frontier' being conquered. Who should have the commercial rights to this information? With the availability of all this information it is now possible to test for many genetic diseases. Should people be compelled to take such tests? Who should have access to the results? What about employers or prospective spouses? Should a 'prevention is better than cure philosophy be employed', i.e. should we decide to prevent parents from passing the gene on to their children or employ 'gene therapies'?

Clearly the advances achieved in the Human Genome Project open up exciting possibilities in terms of the prevention of hereditary disease. In the main the scientists working on the project are prompted by a desire to locate the genes that cause hereditary illness, examine those genes and, with that knowledge, seek out a preventative. Some diseases with a genetic component, such as cancer and heart disease, can be screened for and although there are no cures, preventive measures such as dietary restrictions and chemical treatment can be taken. Moreover, patients with serious genetic diseases have no other hope for an improvement in their situation. Who can say that they should be denied this hope?

The difficulty is that this knowledge also has the potential to be abused and brings new ethical questions. As Steve Jones points out: 'Genetics also presents a more subtle and more universal dilemma – the problem of knowledge. Soon, it will tell many of us how and when we are likely to die. Already, it is possible to diagnose at birth genes which will kill in childhood, youth or early middle age.... Will people really want to know that they are at risk of a disease about which they can do nothing? ... The greatest dilemma of all will be that of being aware of our own fate or that of our offspring.'[6] On a human and clinical level this new knowledge of the chromosomes which contribute to various diseases and disabilities will raise many difficult dilemmas for doctors. Should a practitioner inform patients that they are susceptible to the onset of a hereditary disease in later life, even if, at the present stage of the research, nothing can be done about that disease? This new knowledge may raise awkward questions about the duties and meaning of parenthood.

Moreover, while this new knowledge will enable us to delete genes it will also enable us to add genetic attributes. Would it not be desirable for people's self-esteem to add genes to give height to short people, hair to the bald or better eyesight to the myopic? Is it acceptable to insert genes for athleticism or intelligence? Where do we draw the line? Our answers to these questions will be determined by our understanding of the value of the individual in society and about the appropriate use of scarce health resources.

Genetic imperialism
Ruth Hubbard and Elijah Wald argue that the mindset which propels the Human Genome Project is reductionism at its most extreme, claiming that it illustrates a flawed view of genes being 'all powerful' in determining human disease and behaviour.[7] In this perspective, far from revealing what it is to be human, this venture will reduce the essence of humanity to a hypothetical sequence of sub-microscopic pieces of DNA molecules.

They go on to argue that DNA functions are often overstated, particularly when scientists use terminology like 'controlling', 'programming' or 'determining' traits in relation to DNA. Their point is that these verbs are all inappropriate because they assign far too active a role to DNA, conveying the impression that segments of DNA are absolute predictors. While a functional DNA sequence does of course have a significant role to play, it is not necessarily the only one of the components that participate in engendering a particular trait. It is easy shorthand to call such sequences 'genes'.

Richard Lewontin, Professor of Zoology at Harvard University, takes a similar stance and observes:

> While the talk is of sequencing the human genome, every human differs from every other. The DNA I got from my mother differs by about one tenth of one per cent from the DNA I got from my father, and I differ by about that much from any other human being. The final catalogue of "the" human DNA sequence will be a mosaic of some hypothetical average person corresponding to no one.[8]

According to Lewontin, by magnifying the mythic importance our culture attaches to heredity and in particular by increasingly appropriating the right to define what is 'normal' in human biology and behaviour, proponents of the Human Genome Project run the risk of imposing a 'new eugenics' upon society.

Lewontin goes on to observe that the problem of establishing direct causality between specific genes and specific traits is further complicated by the fact that 'messages' carried by specific DNA sequences vary in different contexts, in the same way as words have different meanings in different contexts. He uses an analogy with the many meanings of the word 'do':

> No word in English has more powerful implications of action than 'do'. 'Do it now!' Yet in most of the contexts, 'do' as in 'I do not know' is periphrastic, and has no meaning at all. While the periphrastic 'do' has no meaning, it undoubtedly has a linguistic function as a place holder and spacing element in the arrangement of a sentence ... So elements in the genetic message may have meaning, or they may be periphrastic. The

[DNA] sequence 'GTAAGT' is sometimes read by the cell as an instruction to insert the amino acids valine and serine in a protein, but sometimes it signals a place where the cell machinery is to be cut up and edit the message; and sometimes it may be only a spacer ... that keeps other parts of the message at an appropriate distance from each other. Unfortunately, we do not know how the cell decides among the possible interpretations.[9]

There has long been a dispute whether heredity or environment have greater significance. Even Shakespeare got in on the act. In *The Tempest* Prospero describes Caliban as 'A devil, a born devil, on whose nature Nurture can never stick'. As we saw in the previous chapter belief in the power of heredity was strong at the beginning of this century. Nazism turned people off eugenics but must also stand as a horrific warning of the dangers of assigning too much power to biological inheritance. To overstate the importance of genes is to attempt to provide simple answers to complicated questions. The complex interactions and transformations that go on inside us, and between us and our environment, are too sophisticated to be carved into simplistic patterns. We are not just the sum of our genes. Our environment is full of other living organisms, ranging from the bacteria that colonise our intestines and supply us with essential vitamins and other foodstuffs, to the human beings and other animals with whom we live. No study of our genetic disposition can by itself unlock the key to our 'human nature'. In response to the suggestion that alcoholism is a genetic disorder Abby Lippman observes:

Most generally, calling something 'genetic' directs us to look inward for the underlying gene(s), privileges this component in isolation from others, and makes alcoholism separate from the context in which people do and do not become alcoholic.

It shifts our vision from person to the lab. Even more worrisome, it evokes consideration of all the technologies and services thought to be appropriate for those dealing with a 'genetic' problem, such as screening to find carriers, prenatal testing to identify those 'at risk', or gene manipulation to fix faulty genes.[10]

In much of the genetic discussion nature wins out in the debate with nurture. People become personally responsible for 'causing' their disease and for preventing it. Yet the cause of disease is multifactorial, and such language is inflated way beyond the actual explanatory power of genetics. To put too much stress on the genetics dimension is to fail to do justice to the other factors that influence our health.

Of course this raises the question of what we understand by health. Is the goal of 'genetic medicine' to relieve pain and suffering, or to enhance the human condition? This in turn raises the question of how we see the goal of medicine: to care or to cure? Does the genetic-driven approach view health in terms of the optimal functioning of our biological organisms or of the person as a whole? If that is the case does that mean that the goals of medicine require us to pursue every possible genetic therapy?

Voices in the genetic wilderness
A number of dissenting voices have been raised about the underlying premise of some of the champions of the Human Genome Project and of the increasing use of techniques like genetic screening who assume that there is a relatively simple relationship between genes and human characteristics. Inherited conditions like eye colour involve an extremely complex interplay of many factors and processes, and cannot be reduced to single genes acting alone. As we saw in chapter 2, genetic information was initially gleaned from Mendel's experiments with tall and short pea plants. There is

a risk that we may forget that a pea plant with tall genes, receiving inadequate sunlight, water or nutrients, will be short.[11]

Taken to extremes, the 'all-powerful gene' may contribute to social discrimination. Richard Lewontin claims that the Human Genome Project will have far-reaching implications:

> The medical model that begins, for example, with a genetic explanation of the extensive and irreversible degeneration of the central nervous system characteristic of Huntington's Chorea, may end with an explanation of human intelligence, of how much people drink, how intolerable they find the social condition of their lives, whom they chose as sexual partners, and whether they get sick on the job. A medical model of all human variation makes a medical model of normality, including social normality, and dictates a therapeutic or preemptive attack on deviance.[12]

Evelyn Fox Keller is particularly concerned that the Human Genome Project distinguishes a 'eugenics of normalcy' by ensuring that each individual has a sufficient amount of normal genes since people have a paramount right to be born with a normal, adequate hereditary endowment. She sees the current concern with 'disease-causing genes' as a 1990s version of the 'new eugenics' particularly in the light of the ever-growing list of conditions characterised as 'genetic disease'.[13]

A particular area of concern is the use of predictive tests for 'learning disabilities' which may not do justice to the uncertainties inherent in such trials and may not address their underlying assumptions. Norms generate deviance, and an 'abnormal result' on a biological or genetic test, while not attaching blame on children, stigmatises them and projects that stigma into the future. Such diagnostic labels can have a devastating effect on a child's self-image and could seriously impair their relationships in school or at home. In our computer age records of these characteristics will inevitably follow a child from school to school or from employer to employer. Moreover, the relatives and especially the descendants of those with so-called 'genetic learning disabilities' may share the stigma.

Social scientists have insightfully observed that the use of diagnostic techniques has substantial social force beyond the educational context. The school system has traditionally been responsible for assessing, categorising and channelling children toward future roles. Accordingly, teachers could be forced to transmit their evaluations to other institutions to help identify who is genetically constituted to assume certain types of jobs. In this way diagnostic technologies not only help schools meet their own internal needs, they also empower schools in their role as gatekeepers for the larger society.[14]

These social scientists are concerned that genes take on a life of their own and could be used to explain why poor children do not perform 'up to the required standard' in school and even why their families are poor in the first place and will always be poor. The danger is that genes will provide an easy scapegoat and absolve society from any culpability in this situation.

In this context the remarks of molecular biologist and editor-in-chief of *Science* magazine, D. E. Koshland, are particularly noteworthy. He speculates about the use of genetic therapy to assist certain forms of IQ deficiencies and poses the question: 'If a child destined to have a permanently low IQ could be cured by replacing a gene, would anyone really argue against that?' I am not so sure, in the light of the eugenical undertones of this statement. However, the most chilling aspect of this question is his use of the word 'cured' in relation to a low IQ. This kind of mindset sends the ethical alarm bells into overdrive.

Koshland goes on to speculate: 'Is there an argument against making superior individuals? Not superior morally, and not superior philosophically, just superior in certain skills: better at computers, better as musicians, better physically. As society gets more complex, perhaps it must select individuals more capable of coping with its complex problems.'[15]

This line of thought brings us into the ethical red light zone where scientists, or other self-appointed referees of human excellence, will identify the point of demarcation between 'bad' genes and 'good' ones. What criteria are to be used in this process of unnatural selection? Political? Economic? Scientific? Ethical? If so, whose ethics?

The PR battle

The proponents of the Human Genome Project have won an important public relations battle in convincing a large chunk of public opinion that ill health can be viewed primarily as a genetic problem. By putting priority on our genetic disposition, inadequate attention is often given to environmental and social factors.

Hubbard and Wald illustrate the allocative dimension of this question with the example of the search for a 'gene for diabetes'.[16] Diabetes is a disturbance of carbohydrate metabolism, marked by much higher than normal concentrations of the sugar glucose in the blood. Two forms of diabetes can be distinguished – somewhat unimaginatively known as Type 1 and Type 2. Type 1 diabetes tends to strike during adolescence, though it can start earlier or later, and it begins quite suddenly. Type 2, the more prevalent form, usually creeps up gradually and, as a norm, not until people have passed middle age.

The metabolic patterns which underlie the two forms are quite different. Type 1 diabetes results from the destruction of cells in the pancreas that usually generate insulin, a hormone involved in glucose metabolism. This type is considered to involve the immune system and be the result of an allergic response to toxic chemicals in the environment, a viral infection, or another unidentified stimulus. In marked contrast people with Type 2 diabetes secrete normal or above-normal amounts of insulin, but their tissues develop an insensitivity to it. Consequently the insulin loses its metabolic effectiveness. Type 2 can frequently be alleviated by a diet low in carbohydrates and fats, especially in conjunction with moderate levels of exercise. One study of six thousand middle-aged men established that regular exercise, such as jogging, cycling and swimming, significantly reduced the incidence of Type 2 diabetes. Of course this is not to preclude the possibility that Type 2 diabetes has a genetic component but to illustrate that other factors enter into the equation.[17]

Molecular biologists contend that several proteins are involved in the development of Type 2 diabetes and are at present seeking to track down and examine the genes that specify the amino acid sequences of insulin and an 'insulin receptor'. When sufficient information is known about the structure and location of these two genes, scientists will then be in a position to detect differences in their base sequences. Those tests could then be used to predict a 'predisposition' to develop Type 2 diabetes in healthy people who are members of families where this condition occurs. The objective of this study is to develop a predictive test for a 'predisposition' to develop a condition that large numbers of people could prevent by recourse to a healthier diet and lifestyle. Does it not therefore make more economic and common sense to use those scarce resources on education and to work towards providing the economic and social conditions that could enable more people to live healthily, instead of ploughing considerable resources into finding 'aberrant' genes and to identify those people whose genetic constitution puts them at special risk?

The susceptibility to Type 1 diabetes seems to cluster in families and in specific populations, for example Northern Europeans. If one child in the family has Type 1 diabetes, the probability of a brother or sister developing it is approximately 6 per cent, about twenty times the incidence in the population at large. Although this might suggest a genetic component, it is also significant that an identical twin of a person who develops Type 1 has only a 36 per cent probability of developing the condition. Not surprisingly this is higher than the probability for 'ordinary' siblings but it also conclusively establishes that genes are not the only determining factor. While toxic environmental agents and viral infections are considered to trigger off Type 1 diabetes, family correlations need not point to a genetic origin. Siblings who reside together tend to be exposed to the same environmental agents. Molecular biologists are currently attempting to develop predictive genetic tests for this condition. They are not examining an 'insulin gene' but genes that participate in the synthesis of proteins active in immune reactions. Hubbard and Wald see this enterprise as a pointless drain on resources because the results of such predictive diagnoses will be tentative at best in view of the complexities of the immune system and because no one knows what factors trigger this particular immune response. Moreover, the test will do nothing to reduce exposure to the toxic chemicals that have been linked to the condition.[18] The example of the search for a gene for diabetes raises a fundamental question about the Human Genome Project: could it deflect attention from more important issues?

Conclusion
According to Pascal: 'All human troubles arise from an unwillingness to stay where we were born.' This approach is excessively pessimistic. The opponents of the Human Genome Project see it as a threat on the basis that to interfere with our inheritance is a curse for the future. It should be recognised that the new genetic knowledge has brought little but benefit to date. One question which must be confronted is: Is the vast expense justified? The health dividend will be enormous in terms of the number of

new drugs that will be available. The Human Genome Project could be seen as a means to an end – to help the human community to interfere in our evolutionary development in order to better the individual and the human species. Perhaps it also raises important methodological issues for ethics particularly about 'means' and 'ends'. The developed world has a rich tradition of ethical reflection about ends but a comparatively impoverished one about means. Perhaps the Human Genome Project will provide the impetus for this situation to be reversed. The new genetic knowledge represents great possibilities but it also brings problems. These problems are insufficient reason to stop the study but they do present us with a challenge to use our creativity to ensure that genetic information is used for human betterment. The initial ethical challenge is to arrive at an adequate understanding of 'human betterment'. Let us make haste slowly.

4

THE GENETIC DETECTIVES

Every parent-to-be is understandably concerned with the question: 'Will my baby be healthy?' Up to recent times genetic screening has not been a practical option because of the expense and because most detectable conditions were quite rare. Now that situation has been transformed. Scanning equipment developed to examine the three-thousand-year-old mummified body of an Egyptian priestess without damaging her has been adapted to detect abnormalities of babies in the womb. The technique was developed by Dr Stephen Hughes after he had been asked by the British Museum in 1991 to examine 'Jeni', who lived in the twenty-second dynasty. He used a scanner which produced a series of cross-sectional images revealing details of her heart and other organs without unwrapping the body and causing damage. He discovered that she was probably no more than twenty years old when she died but he was unable to discover the cause of her death. The London-based doctor subsequently adapted this ultra-sound technique to scan mothers-to-be.

An important milestone in genetic screeening was reached in 1990 with the isolation of the cystic fibrosis gene. The cost of this enterprise was $150,000,000, though with technical advances the cost of finding other genes will be much less. Cystic fibrosis is the most frequently inherited abnormality among white-skinned people; in Europe about one child in 2,500 is affected. Already, early diagnosis and treatment can extend the lifespan significantly.

An economic dimension is sometimes brought into the discussion; testing for a disease such as cystic fibrosis costs about £2,000 compared with £14,000 to £20,000 annually in treatment for every one of the seven thousand sufferers in the UK. The theory is that if people knew, for example, they had the gene for alcoholism they might avoid alcohol. Equally if they knew they had a gene for heart disease they could practise prevention by changing their diet and lifestyle. In this perspective genetic screening is a cost-efficient way of treating illness.

There are currently about seven thousand known genetic disorders and about twenty new genes are being reported weekly. We all have between one and three abnormal genes. Each of us has a genetic burden. For some it is uncovered because they suffer from a disease caused by it, e.g. Marfan's Syndrome (a condition, which supposedly affected Abraham Lincoln and Rachmaninov, in which an individual grows very tall and thin with long fingers and suffers heart complaints). In other cases it is unearthed when a person has a genetic test. As more is discovered about the genetic causes of various diseases, it is becoming obvious that even a common disease like cancer has elements of a genetic disorder. The diseases which affect people are cast in our DNA from the time of our conception. Our parents' genes predetermine our fates before our first heartbeat.

Sophisticated new techniques have emerged for examining chromosomes including 'FISH' (Fluorescence In Situ Hybridisation), which uses colour probes to paint chromosomes, each of which may contain up to five thousand genes, in order that anomalies may be detected. Searching for missing pieces or pieces which have been swapped around in chromosomes, it could diagnose disorders such as Prader-Willi syndrome, in which a piece of chromosome is missing and children are mentally disabled, floppy as babies and later very obese, with an obsession for food. 'Gene testing' examines the DNA that encodes or makes up the gene itself.

Parents or potential parents who carry genes for disabilities, mental or physical, understandably seek to learn their risks of having affected children. Prenatal diagnosis of genetic defects is increasingly available, so that parents worried about Down's Syndrome might request their obstetricians to conduct amniocentesis, where samples of the amniotic fluid surrounding the foetus in the womb will be tested. Establishing that a foetus has a genetic defect enables parents to prepare themselves psychologically for the birth. Some parents in this situation may consider the option of an abortion.

Behind genetic closed doors
In its broadest sense genetic screening refers to a study of the occurrence of persons with a specific gene or chromosome composition in a population or population group. There are three main reasons why genetic screening may be resorted to. Firstly, to identify people with a gene or chromosome composition which may result in, or predispose the people concerned, to develop a disease. Secondly, to identify people with a gene or chromosome composition which may result in, or predispose their offspring to develop a disease. Thirdly, to establish the frequency of a given genetic disease, a specific chromosomal rearrangement or possibly a specific combination of genes in the population.

Prenatal and even preconceptual screening can identify many problems through amniocentesis, ultrasound, and other tests which detect conditions for which prenatal interventions are available. There is the problem of the absence of treatment, other than abortion, for many of the problems the screening identifies. To date there has been some discussion about the ethics of prenatal screening for HIV infection, while some health professionals advocate elective screening for identification of foetal gender.

New genetic knowledge brings new potential. Understanding a particular disease is an essential prerequisite for treating it. At the moment genetics can do more than just test for abnormalities – it can treat some inborn diseases. Children born with phenylketonuria, the inability to metabolise a certain amino acid, tended to die young in the past. Now a diet which excludes the amino acid means that the child born with the condition can live a fairly normal life. While other therapies for inherited illness are more complicated, they can work just as well, for example the injection of a blood-clotting factor cures the symptoms of haemophilia.

Baby Chloe

The plus side of the genetic revolution is illustrated in the experience of a Lancashire couple Paul and Michelle O'Brien. Their baby, Martin, was born with cystic fibrosis, a terminal disease that retards growth. Neither had known they carried the gene for the condition. In the face of Martin's almost certain death as a young man because of the disease, and the risk of passing the condition on to their next child they decided never to risk another pregnancy. Even if the foetus could be screened, they would still be confronted with the trauma of waiting for test results and the daunting prospect of several abortions before they produced a healthy embryo. As both were carriers of the gene their prospective children had a one-in-four chance of having the disease.

By accident the O'Briens discovered a revolutionary alternative. They could undergo IVF treatment at the pioneering Hammersmith Hospital in West London where a number of eggs could be fertilised in one operation and researchers would sift through the resulting embryos, selecting one or two healthy ones for implantation in the womb. The rest would be discarded. This process of discarding embryos raises ethical questions of its own.

The result of the O'Briens' treatment was Chloe, the first baby in the world to be born after screening for a specific defective gene. During the pregnancy the couple refused tests to check whether the embryo selection had been successful. They had decided in advance that they did not want to have an abortion if Chloe had cystic fibrosis and there was a risk that tests might cause Michelle to have a miscarriage. After Chloe was born blood tests revealed that she did not have the disease. Within a two-year period the number of children worldwide who had been born using the same procedures had risen to forty – half of them from embryos selected at Hammersmith.

In 1994 one of Britain's leading infertility specialists, Professor Robert Winston, revealed that his Hammersmith team had screened embryos for thirteen gene defects, an advance that could conceivably lead to the virtual elimination of some diseases. Rare single gene-defect conditions such as Tay Sachs disease, which causes death in infancy, or thalassaemia, a form of anaemia that may generate physical retardation, have been identified by embryo selection. However, genetic screening can also bring problems of its own. Steve Jones claims:

> To some, all this is the first step towards Frankenstein. Many of these fears are exaggerated. Most treatments of inherited disease are not very different from those in the rest of medicine … a society which accepts a heart-lung transplant for a child with a cystic fibrosis cannot deny it the right to have the symptoms treated at source with a working gene. All that is different is the level of intervention – the DNA itself rather than what it produces.[1]

The ambigous nature of some genetic knowledge is indicated in the following family case history.

One family's story

When Paul's wife, Mary (not their real names), reached her early forties she began to become irritable and agitated. Psychiatrists initially diagnosed 'pathological anger'. Later the diagnosis was changed to Alzheimer's disease, but Paul had doubts when Mary did not follow the normal course of the condition. Subsequently Paul had Mary tested for Huntington's disease. His horror at learning the positive test result was greatly magnified by the fact that his six adult daughters, who had watched their mother's inexorable decay, had a fifty:fifty chance of having inherited the disease. Not only that but they would have to face similar odds of passing it on to their children. His four married daughters decided to take the test to help decide if they should have any more children or not. Two, Nell and Geraldine, tested positive. Nell faced the dilemma of whether or not to tell her own children. Geraldine had been planning to start a family but decided not to.

Huntington's disease leads to the erosion of the nervous system and death in early middle age. It was originally known as Huntington's Chorea (a word with the same root as choreography) because of the involuntary dancing movements of those struck down by the disease. One eighteenth-century Harvard professor even suggested that the victims of this affliction were blasphemers as their gestures were imitations of the movements of Christ on the Cross.

No one under the age of eighteen can be tested for ethical reasons because there is no cure for Huntington's disease and therefore no advantage in knowing you will develop it without having the emotional and psychological resources to handle the results. Two clinic visits are required before the test can be completed. In the first, Huntington's is explained and the doctor talks through the implications of the test with the patient, such as considering how family and friends will be affected etc. One month later, this process is repeated. If the patient still wants the test, blood is taken. However, before the result is given, the patient must return to the clinic and go through a further session in which the implications of a positive and negative result are considered.

It has been argued that a positive result is on a par with handing a healthy person a death sentence. It is noteworthy that according to an American survey conducted before the test for Huntington's was developed found that 70 per cent of those at risk said they would take the test. After the test was discovered only 17 per cent of those at risk said they would take it.

Prospective parents are already seeking advice on family planning, sterilisation, IVF, genetic testing of test-tube foetuses, artificial insemination by donor, prenatal diagnosis and abortion of severely defective foetuses. New support services are required to provide genetic counselling, prenatal diagnosis and genetic screening for common defects. Should parents be truthful with their children about the conditions which they may inherit? Screening enables individuals to make more informed choices but it may bring more heartache. It is imperative that an adequate counselling system for those at risk of genetic disease be established. Equally there is a need to provide ongoing emotional and psychological support for people who receive the results they do not want to hear.

Genesis revisted

As the Human Genome Project gains momentum new ethical questions will arise in genetic screening. Kathleen Nolan begins her critique of the study by quoting Genesis 3:6:

> And when the woman saw that the tree was good for food, and that it was pleasant to the eyes, and a tree to be desired to make one knowledgeable, she took of the fruit thereof, and did eat, and gave also unto her husband with her; and he did eat.[2]

She points out that one of the first fruits of the Human Genome Project will be many markers for traits and diseases believed to have a genetic base but to date lacking an identified gene or genes. Most of these markers can be developed into diagnostic tests which greatly extends the range of potentially available genetic diagnostic options. However, with the sheer volume of genetic information that will come available there are serious questions about the extent and speed with which these new markers should move from the laboratory bench into various clinical uses. An area of particular concern is modern obstetric practice where increased diagnostic surveillance can change the character and mood of pregnancy, and the need for special caution about increased prenatal genetic testing.

Nolan develops the biblical adage still further by recalling that when Adam and Eve ate of the fruit of the tree of knowledge of good and evil, they were evicted from the Garden of Eden and entered a world of misery. Nolan wonders if the same situation will obtain with the genetics revolution because we now have access to genetic information about ourselves and our offspring that was previously shrouded in mystery. Whether or not we will ultimately benefit from this new knowledge is far from clear. Accordingly, we must consider very carefully 'in what manner and how deeply we will taste the genome project's tempting fruits'.

With the Human Genome Project the options in the area of genetic screening will increase enormously. It is likely that there will be tests for most major, early onset genetic diseases caused by a single gene, but also new genetic information. Genetic screening brings fresh questions – both medical and ethical. Who are such tests for – the parents so that they will gain information about the pregnancy and subsequent children, or the offspring, foetal, embryonic, or pre-embryonic? Does screening contribute to increased anxiety about pregnancy? What are the risks associated with follow-up testing? Are there any social implications of allowing parents prospectively to evaluate their offspring in this fashion? There is also the issue of the accuracy of the procedure. Genetic diagnosis is complex and the vast new information from genomic studies could lead to premature conclusions.

Ethically there is a proliferation of difficult questions. How are the benefits and burdens of testing to be evaluated? Whose interests should be considered in making such an evaluation – that of the parents, the offspring, society, the health care professionals or geneticists? What limits, if any, need to be placed on the availability of such tests? Do we need legislation to regulate the use of information which these tests will generate? How is complex genetic information to be used in making decisions about pregnancies, including the option for abortion? As we have already documented the Human Genome Project opens up great commercial possibilities and there will be considerable pressure to introduce new diagnostic tests quickly in order to secure patents on the new techniques that will make testing a more routine part of prenatal care. Who will assess the new services and procedures?

In the US context, for example, the Food and Drug Administration includes formal testing in the process for licensing new drugs, but its jurisdiction over and interest in viewing diagnostic tests arising from the Human Genome Project are unclear. In a litigation culture will fearful clinicians seek to reduce their perceived threat of liability by offering the broadest possible panel of diagnostic tests? Perhaps this threat highlights the need for a debate on which tests should be considered important, optional or unnecessary. Clearly advances in genetic knowledge need to be complemented by advances in the education of the laity about how to use this education effectively. Who will pay for such screening? Are people who are unable to pay to be denied access to screening? It will shortly be possible to test a large section of the population for genetic predisposition to a wide range of cancers, respiratory diseases and cardiovascular disorders, diabetes, alcoholism and schizophrenia. This means that widespread specialist genetic counselling services are essential. But are they available?

Kathleen Nolan points out that the ethics of prenatal genetic counselling require that prospective parents be provided with full information and then be allowed to choose which, if any, genetic diagnostic tests to pursue. The ideal is value-neutral counselling and autonomous decision-making. The achievement of this ideal is problematic except where well-trained counsellors are available and affordable, and where counsellors and clients share a common cultural background:

> Yet the demands of routine prenatal care make it difficult simply to transpose this ethical framework into the obstetric or primary care clinic. The volume of patients is large, there is little enough time as it is to attend to patients' psychological needs, and there are frequently quite prominent gaps between the social and cultural backgrounds of prenatal health care professionals and their patients. Moreover, genetic counsellors have in the past generally been able, based on specific clinical indications, to focus their attention on one disease or syndrome at a time, while in the future, decision-making will likely encompass a broad spectrum of conditions for which prospective parents may be at no particular increased risk.[3]

High-tech genetics

Having considered the area of genetic screening on a general level it is necessary to examine more specific aspects of the issue. Embryo biopsy gives couples the opportunity of signing on with an IVF programme and transferring to the uterus only embryos deemed free from the 'genetic flaw'. Embryos can also be sexed in order to transfer only female embryos to prospective mothers at risk of passing a sex-linked genetic disease like Duchenne muscular dystrophy. For this reason one paediatrician likened embryo diagnosis to the 'ultimate measles vaccine'. His argument was that if we vaccinate children to prevent the spread of disease within a generation, should we not also discard embryos to avoid passing disease between generations? Screening of embryos allows a deleterious recessive gene to be eliminated from a family's genetic line as part of the attempt to prevent disease by correcting genetic defects in embryos. Embryo therapy will prevent disease in a different way by treating genetic anomalies in embryos and then protecting and transferring the embryos. However, many things are still unknown in this whole area. Three important questions need to be confronted as a matter of urgency. What needs are answered by embryo genetics? Is this the most appropriate way of responding to those needs? Should our society give priority to these needs? Andrea Bonnicksen's observes:

> Beneath the excitement of embryo genetics lie fears that are shunted aside rather than confronted – the fear of having a child with an anomaly, the fear of having disabled children in the society, and practitioners' fear of being left behind if they do not add embryo genetics to their list of services. Various needs are being cloaked by the addition of a new set of reproductive technologies. The impetus for the new genetics does not seem to be coming from groups of at-risk couples, but instead from intrigue over the promise of genetic inquiry.[4]

Recent advances in embryo diagnosis pose ethical problems. The key question is: if something becomes technically possible, it is therefore ethically responsible? In many cases the answer is yes. At other times though the answer must be no because a particular technique is found to be against human dignity and at variance with the true purpose of medicine itself, which is to be of service to the human person as a whole. What has happened is not so much that the scientists and medical personnel involved have been unconcerned about whether or not they were making responsible use of their knowledge and skill. The real problem is that mutually inconsistent forms of ethical evaluation have come into play, but this inconsistency, and the inadequacy of some of the approaches have not being recognised. This situation urgently needs to be corrected because, as Bonnicksen remarks perceptively:

> Embryo diagnosis is a rapidly changing technology being introduced quietly in the clinical setting. The technology will ultimately affect the genetic composition of future humans, and it creates a new specialty at a time when discrepancies in medical treatment between rich and poor are entrenched and growing. It brings the yearning to control the life course to a point so early in development that it negates the value of chance in everyday life.[5]

There are also wider issues. Is this current focus on finding the genetic causes of disease a distraction from other important questions, for example the effort to screen workers with vulnerable genes rather than ridding the workplace of hazardous chemicals? This approach is ethically dubious because the focus is on keeping potentially sick people out of the population rather than on preventing members of that population from becoming sick.

Do all parents want or need to know what grief is in store for their offspring? Do they need to know how they are most likely to suffer or to die, or when? More can be done to control the destiny of humankind with social, economic, environmental and political change than with the most sophisticated embryo diagnosis.

Testing positive
Moving from the specific to the general there are two obvious, potentially adverse effects of genetic screening. Firstly, there are the possible effects on the person concerned. 'Normality' is a relative

concept, and any health-related examination includes a risk of the subjects feeling or being thought of as abnormal or just ill, as, for example, in the case of foetal screening for chromosomal disorders, where secondary findings in the form of chromosonal deviations of a relatively minor nature might cause the prospective parents to have a prejudiced attitude towards the abnormal status of an expected child. Detection of genetic carrier status in the form of disposition to a disease might cause people to think of themselves as seriously ill, with a resulting disproportionate and gloomy influence on a person's *joie de vivre.* Genetic screening increases the chances of detecting diseases or dispositions long before they may have actual implications for health, as in the case of Huntington's disease, where more than forty years may elapse between the detection of the trait and the outbreak of the disease. This may cause the people affected to feel that their life is predetermined.

Secondly, there is a community dimension. Just as people may consider themselves 'abnormal' the detection of certain genetic traits could cause sections of the population to have prejudiced attitudes towards certain genetic carriers. Society tends to lay down norms stating which attributes are desirable and which are not, and there is a danger that some people may be discriminated against. This is best illustrated by an example. Sickle-cell anaemia is a disease which is prevalent in Africa, parts of India, the Middle East and among Afro-Americans. Individuals with two genes for sickle-cell anaemia display symptoms in the form of anaemia and small blood clots. A person with just one sickle-cell gene is a carrier of the disease, which is recessively transmitted in the same way as cystic fibrosis. In the US an effort was made to conduct genetic screening to locate Afro-American carriers of sickle-cell anaemia. The purpose of the screening was to give at-risk couples the option of deciding not to have to children, as there were insufficient facilities then for foetal diagnosis. Since screening was carried out on Afro-Americans only, many deemed it to be racist.

The firm

Employers are anxious to have their staff disclose any genetic traits that may make them more susceptible to hazards at work since such information may absolve management of responsibility for contributing to workers' disease. Although some firms may be unwilling to exclude workers, insurers may 'encourage' them to collect genetic information and to differentiate between high-risk and low-risk people. As genetic information becomes ever more prevalent many more people will find themselves stigmatised as bad employment risks. This is particularly an issue in the case of high-paying jobs.

The Johnson Controls case decided by the Supreme Court in 1991 is a timely reminder of how genetic information is used to identify high-risk groups. The battery manufacturers, Johnson Controls, had a policy of excluding women of child-bearing age from high-paying jobs involving exposure to lead because they feared that such exposure might damage foetuses. The company also feared a lawsuit from a woman who claimed to have been damaged in this way. The firm excluded all women from such positions unless they could prove they had been surgically sterilised. The Supreme Court, in a unanimous decision, decided that it is unlawful discrimination to ban all women of child-bearing age from specific jobs because of possible foetal damage.

One of the interesting features of the case was that it was only women who were being excluded from lead exposure, even though there is strong evidence of the damage to that lead causes to all adults, and evidence of damage to children whose fathers have been exposed.

The inevitability of the increased use of computers in the clinical setting raises questions about the confidentiality of genetic records. Because genetic information can so easily be stored electronically, patient privacy may be more routinely violated as insurers, employers and government investigators scan computerised databases.

Individuals at high risk will almost certainly face discrimination. Sensitive genetic information could be abused by powerful groups. Could the future be a world where mortgages are not provided to high risk groups or even where couples expect prospective partners to disclose their risk of dementia prior to marriage?

New genetic tests do not have to be licensed or undergo trials. Could such tests ultimately be used to screen for selective breeding? Studies are already under way for the assessment of genetic influences on personality and intelligence. Where do we draw the line in this area? Do we wait for problems to manifest themselves before we put appropriate legislation in place or do we legislate in advance? As genes associated with desirable characteristics are isolated it is virtually certain there will be a resurgence of interest in selective breeding. Parents might reject pre-implantation diagnosis because of the additional risks from the drugs that stimulate the ovaries to produce many eggs at once. It seems more likely that many couples will opt for genetic screening with the possibility of abortion in certain circumstances.

The example of so-called 'test-tube' babies is worth noting. In the UK context, for example, there were sixteen years of discussion before the first regulatory body was established to oversee IVF treatment, and it is often the case that in the whole area of reproductive technology legislation is lagging way behind social reality. History should teach us that we will pay a high price for sitting back passively waiting for the thorny ethical questions to arise in genetic screening.

In the immediate future our fates will be read in our genes. This brings its own risks. Already in the US insurance companies are practising an ugly form of genetic discrimination by screening out genes for various disorders. If this were to become common practice people would invariably be subjected to a proliferation of genetic tests before they could be insured.

Significant numbers of people are denied access to health care on the basis of their past medical history. Genetic testing may take us in to a minefield. Should an insurance company have the right to see the results of genetic tests to enable them to decide whether or not to insure the person in question? Is a 'defective' gene a pre-existing condition? Health insurance is based on spreading risk. Genetics shatters our ignorance of future disease. Accordingly, no one would want to pay for health cover if they think they will have a long and healthy life and will not need it. Equally, if an insurance company knows that an expensive illness is inevitable given the person's genetic disposition their premiums will go through the roof.

The director of Communication for the American Council for Life Insurance has stated that he wished 'that genetic technology had never been developed'. This raises the question of whether we should consider a national health service, which spreads individual risk throughout the population at large.

There is evidence, particularly in the US, that some companies are refusing to insure those who will fall prey to Huntington's disease. In America a woman was denied insurance because her children had symptoms of this disease, although she herself had none. In an environment where employers pay the cost of their employees' insurance they may be reluctant to employ people in the high risk category. This of course raises very big questions for society. Could we have genetic apartheid? Dr Richard Nicholson, editor of the *Bulletin of Medical Ethics* remarked: 'A baby carrying a genetic defect which will be fatal within a few years is not the same as one that would be fatal in later life. We run the risk of trying to improve the general standard of human stock by genetics.'

For your eyes only

The availability of sensitive information about a person's genes raise larger questions about the use of sensitive personal data in administrative systems. It can, at least potentially, be used by 'authorities' to supervise, limit and control the individual's behaviour. There could be a risk of people's integrity being violated, either when recording and using data or when disseminating sensitive information to other authorities who intend to use it for other purposes. From a protective perspective, genetic information differs in two crucial ways from other sensitive health-related information about a person. Firstly, genetic data not only contain information about particular people but can also reveal knowledge about their relatives. It may be shown that these relatives are carriers of a disease or have an illness. Secondly, genetic information provides knowledge of a hitherto unknown magnitude – extremely comprehensive and precise information about the clinical picture of individuals and population groups.

Genetics is currently in a state of extraordinary evolution, chiefly because of the different mapping projects. The level of information will have an impact on key ethical concepts such as consent, autonomy, privacy and integrity. From society's perspective, screening is a cost-efficient way to prevent costly treatment of disease, protecting third-parties and giving the person who proves to be ill the option of treatment. However, from the individual's point of view, screening is far more problematic since it involves people's attitudes to their own or their family's serious illness.

There are two possible ethical responses. Firstly, there is a utilitarian approach – the ethical thinking behind the implementation of screening consists in determining whether the benefit that can be expected is greater than the possible harm. Secondly, there is an approach which safeguards the individual's personal sphere and subjects the knowledge of a disease and the decision on treatment/action to the competent person's right of autonomy. The question at its simplest is: must the principal purpose of applying human genetics be formulated in terms of the gain for the common good or in terms of the individual?

The Helsinki II Declaration on biomedical research on human subjects tilts the balance firmly in favour of the individual:

> Every precaution must be taken to minimise the effect of the research project on the testee's physical and mental integrity and personality ... Regard for the interest of the researchee must always be put before the interests of research or society... In research on humans, research and the interests of society should never take precedence over consideration for the well-being of the testee... The right of the testee to protect his/her integrity must at all times be respected.

As new genetic discoveries continue faster than the ability of the appropriate authorities to regulate them there is increased concern about the ethical dilemmas posed by the boom in screening and the commercial pressures to force it on an unsuspecting public. Where do we draw the line between screening out terminal conditions and those that may allow people a happy and productive though disabled life? What happens as the choice expands from cystic fibrosis to breast cancer to diabetes?

The evidence of history is that in ethical discourse forewarned is not necessarily forearmed. It does not take much imagination to realize that an ethical equivalent of a hornet's nest will arise if a gene test for Alzheimer's disease, the progressive destruction of memory and personality, is discovered. People reaching eighty have a one-in-five chance of developing it, and the ageing population will produce nearly 750,000 sufferers in Britain by 2000. In 1993 American scientists have identified the genetic factors and a risk-predictor test will be on the market by the end of the century. At the moment, as there is no treatment there seems little point in patients having the test.

Screening with a therapeutic end implies a state of tension between three crucially important factors: the public authorities' desire to do all they can to maximise the health status of the community; respect for the individual's personal sphere and autonomy; respect for the other people for whom the individual's disease has implications. How can these principles be reconciled? The World Health Organisation has drawn up a ten-point checklist to be consulted prior to conducting any screening:

1. The disease must constitute a major health problem.
2. There must be an accepted treatment for patients diagnosed as having the disease.
3. Diagnostic and therapeutic facilities must be available.
4. The disease must be demonstrable in a latent or early symptomatic stage.
5. A suitable test or examination method must be available.
6. The test/examination method must be acceptable to the population.
7. The progress of the disease in untreated cases – including development from latent to manifest phases – must have been adequately clarified.
8. The treatment indications must be clearly defined.
9. The cost of detecting the disease (including diagnosis and treatment of patients) must be in reasonable proportion to the health service's total expenditure.
10. The screening action must be an ongoing process, not a one-off phenomenon.

Conclusion

What is urgently required is an approach to ethical questions in this area which will allow us to reason through the problems that arise on the basis of an appreciation of what makes life human; how real human values can be enhanced or jeopardised; how human dignity and rights are nurtured, and how they are assaulted. This approach will consider such principles as free and informed consent; respect for human dignity at all stages of life; adequate previous experimentation on animals, and sufficient benefits to justify the risk of failure. Above all it demands that the professionals involved and all interested parties should come together to formulate a blueprint of how progress in genetic engineering can be compatible with the understanding of a vision of the meaning and purpose of human life. In the interim ethical assessments will, therefore, tend to be tentative, cautious and provisional as further progress is made and refinements of technique emerge.

I would like to suggest the following essential safeguards to prevent abuses of genetic screening:

1. The target group for a particular genetic screening must be given adequate information to ensure that their autonomy is respected and nurtured. Specifically they must informed of the aim, limitations and interpretative options of the research project; available scope for action should any disease be discovered; in what way the data will be stored and to whom it will be available; the genetic situation and its consequences and any uncertainty about the reliability or otherwise of the information.

2. Due consideration must be given to the possible importance for family members of the decision whether or not to participate in genetic screening. Moreover, it must be acknowledged that disease is never simply a matter for an individual. People's diseases will also have an impact on the dealings they have with other people.

3. Genetic counselling must be available to those involved in the screening – at both the investigation and follow-up stages.

4. Sensitive personal information ought not be registered unless informed consent for registration is provided by the relevant people.

5

THE EYES HAVE IT

B ack in 1983 the world was intrigued by its first glimpse of a 'shoat', an animal somewhere between a goat and a sheep, on the cover of the prestigious science weekly, *Nature*. Through genetic engineering we can breed almost anything to order. Before Dolly one of the most celebrated animals in the brave new world of genetics was a mouse with the human ear. The mouse was one of a specially engineered breed which lacks an immune system and which therefore did not reject the human graft. The technique which made this possible was known as 'tissue engineering', the fabrication of body parts using human cells to build the structure. Both the ear and the mouse remained healthy after the operation, encouraging scientists to believe that grafting of such fabricated body parts on to humans will also be successful.

This clearly is a significant breakthrough; after Christian Barnard pioneered the technique of heart transplantation in South Africa in 1967 a major problem emerged in the shape of the frequent rejection of the new organ by the immune system of the recipient. If 'tissue engineering' can be used successfully with human patients, it will overcome the rejection problem because the donor organ will be fabricated from the patients' own cells. However, in the light of the excitement about the breakthrough the ethical questions regarding the use of genetically engineered animals for research purposes did not get the attention they deserve.

Currently, there is a major scientific and financial investment by the EU in gene mapping programmes. The development of molecular genetic markers capable of detecting genetic variation at the DNA level unlocks the door to the mapping not only of the human genome but also that of farm animals. The rapid advances in both molecular and embryo biology have led to the opportunity to develop superior animal genotypes. With the arrival of new information from the gene mapping projects and an enhanced understanding of the physiological control of commercially important traits in farm animals, it will enable us to screen and identify genotypes possessing novel and medically important characteristics. The breeding of dairy cattle to produce lactose-free milk, for instance, would make this important protein source nutritionally acceptable to large numbers of lactose-intolerant humans, especially in the majority world. Likewise, the breeding of cattle to produce milk and meat with less fat or with different fats and more protein would offer significant health advantages to the consumer. Improvements in genetic resistance to disease could significantly reduce both production losses and the current widespread use of antibiotics in animal husbandry, as well as enhancing animal welfare. Moreover, the production of pharmaceutically important proteins in cows' milk could offer a virtually unending supply of these compounds for treatment of genetic diseases such as haemophilia.

Genetic engineering

Genetic engineering involves fundamental alterations of the DNA sequence of living cells by entirely artificial means via *in vitro* fusion of living cells or components of cells: such organisms are termed 'recombinant', and are 'transgenic' where separate natural specices have been crossed. The likelihood of such events occurring in the normal course of evolution is extremely small, since natural mutation rates are insufficient, and behavioural, physical, or geographical barriers usually preclude natural transgenic crosses. Genetic engineering will artificially alter the course and speed of evolution, to an extent previously unimaginable.

One of the problems with the debate to date is that there has been confusion about different terms, so that genetic engineering has been confused with 'eugenics'. Another problem is that some of the critics of genetic engineering simply see it as a device to allow parents to select characteristics in a forthcoming child. This is an excessively and uncritically negative view. As a 1994 editorial in *The Lancet* perceptively observed:

> It is curious how frightened people are of genetic engineering compared with say, child abuse. Genetic engineering has so far damaged no one. By contrast, smoking, AIDS, drugs and alcohol have caused massive damage to children *in utero*. People need to become sufficiently DNA literate.

Greater education and critical discussion in this area is imperative.

The level of DNA illiteracy is perhaps a symptom of a deeper problem – a popular antipathy towards science. Samuel Taylor Coleridge went so far as to claim: 'I believe the souls of five hundred Sir Isaac Newtons would go to the making up of a Shakespeare or a Milton.' By the beginning of the twentieth century disenchantment had increased to such an extent that the Spanish philosopher José Ortega y Gasset could select science as a key cause of modern 'primitivism and barbarism'. He regretted that 'while there are more scientists than ever before, there are far fewer cultured men'.

As science has advanced so too has ignorance. Moreover, it has been argued that ignorance of science has acquired a degree of political correctness. The green movement, blaming science for global pollution, has contributed to this. So too has feminism, which has frequently demonised science as the embodiment of men's will-to-power.[1] However, it is not science that has created problems but its misapplication. Reversing the world's pollution problems requires a scientific component. If the feminist argument is indeed correct it may be that the most constructive answer to the problem is increased involvement in scientific education and research.

An ethics audit

As far back as 1979 John Mahoney was one of the first ethicists to grapple seriously with genetic engieering.[2] His starting-point was that genetic engineering requires a detailed and open-minded assessment. Ethically the challenge is to avoid irresponsible speculation or dogmatic denunciation, and, more positively, to identify the values that contribute to the advancement of humankind. Contemporary society has witnessed sufficient evidence of the destructive and dehumanising power of scientific experimentation and achievement to view it with some caution.

Mahoney went on to argue that it is of course right and proper that scientists should seek greater knowledge, but that this search is not an end in itself. Clearly there is a need for some form of control over genetic manipulation, so that, for example, there would be no danger of new and potentially harmful bacteria escaping to endanger whole populations. Any monitoring body should be as broadly based as possible, taking account of wider insights than merely scientific ones to address the issue of what helps, enhances or protects the inherent value and dignity of the individual human person. As Immanuel Kant forcefully observed, people are an end in themselves, not a means, and ought never to be modified, or fabricated, simply to serve an ulterior purpose. It is equally important in our era of 'accountability and transparency' that such questions are discussed publicly, otherwise unnecessary anxiety will be generated.

A particular source of concern is the potential threat to human dignity posed by the possibility of cloning, or the genetic replication of a living person through substituting the nucleus of a body cell for the nucleus of a fertilised human egg, which will then develop naturally to produce a genetic 'carbon copy' of the donor. Perhaps this disquiet is prompted by the worry that the very identity and privacy of individuals, whether they be the donors or their carbon copies. The closest available parallel to cloning is identical twins but even these have individual differences.

Traditionally ethicists have distinguished between positive (or preventive) and negative genetic medicine – though in practice it may not be easy to identify precisely the point of demarcation between the two. As we have already seen a number of inherited diseases like epilepsy arise from chromosomal abnormality; the objective of preventive genetic medicine is to locate the genetic defect in the body cells and to treat it either chemically or by genetic surgery in such a way that defective or harmful genes are not transmitted to the patient's offspring. Its ultimate objective is to eliminate harmful genes from the human genetic pool and by so doing to eradicate various hereditary diseases.

It might be argued that the genetic controlling of humankind by deleting particular genes from the human genetic pool will in fact diminish the richness and variety of humankind's stock of genes which has survived and flourished through a process of natural selection. The reverse side of this coin is that by availing of the same technology it is also possible not merely to eliminate 'unhealthy' genes but also to introduce and promote what are considered to be desirable genes. However, what do we consider desirable genes to be? Who decides? Who decides who decides?

Ends and means

In 1912 the first Professor of Genetics at Cambridge, William Bateson, in a book called *Biological Fact and the Structure of Society,* argued that: 'the idea of social reform must not be to abolish class, but to ensure that each individual shall as far as possible get into the right class, stay there and usually his children after him.' Eighty years later, in their best-selling *The Bell Curve* (1994), American academics Richard Herrnstein and Charles Murray agreed that status is ruled by biology: 'Success and failure in the American economy are increasingly a matter of the genes that people inherit. ...Programmes to expand opportunities for the disadvantaged are not going to make much difference.' They contend that the poor are to blame for their own situation and speak of 'a high-tech and more lavish version of the Indian reservation for some substantial minority of the nation's population', as the rest of America marches on socially and economically.

In February 1997 the scientist who discovered DNA, Dr James Watson, told the London *Independent* that women should have the right to abort for any reason, including dyslexia, a genetic lack of a musical talent, or even being too short to play basketball. The implication appears to be that if a foetus which has undergone DNA or gene testing is considered to be likely to have 'flaws', the woman may choose to abort and hope that the next pregnancy will lead to a more 'desirable' baby.

In an interview with *The Sunday Telegraph* Watson stated: 'We already accept that most couples don't want a Down's Syndrome child. You would have to be crazy to say that you wanted one, because that child has no future. So to tell a woman she has to look after a Down's baby, to look after a sick child, is like these priests who tell women what to do. Well, they don't have to deal with the reality of it. ...Some day a child is going to sue its parents for being born. They will say: my life is so awful with these terrible genetic defects and you just callously didn't find out. Or you knew and didn't do anything about it.'

Watson went on to argue that parents have a moral responsibility to ensure that their babies are born as healthy as possible. However, his definition of 'healthy' seemed to include an individual's sexual orientation and he appeared to advocate the abortion of foetuses carrying a 'gay gene', lest the babies be pre-disposed towards homosexuality in their adult lives. One of the difficulties of this position is that the so-called 'gay gene' may not even exist. This is not the forum to adjudicate on this scientific controversy but Watson's views seem to mirror those of a consumer society where imperfections of any kind are not to be tolerated.

As we saw in our discussion of eugenics this attitude has led to dangerous consequences and continues to do so. In China, the 1995 law on Maternal and Infant Health Care makes prenatal testing compulsory; this is to be followed by termination if a disorder is found. In 1996 the Irish Medical Organisation Conference adopted a motion rejecting prenatal genetic testing for non-treatable disorders or gender selection, on the grounds that it was discriminatory and constituted a threat to the life of an unborn patient.

Our technological society must be wary of a major ethical problem: that of treating people as laboratory subjects. This temptation permeates the entire spectrum of medical practice, although the danger is perhaps heightened in genetic engineering. In treating a molecule of DNA, we can never forget the actual person nor lose sight of the fact that in dealing with the biological roots of their identity, we are touching them at a more fundamental level.

It is interesting that as far back as 1953 Pope Pius XII, in an address to the First International Symposium of Genetic Medicine pointed out that 'the fundamental tendency of genetics and eugenics is to influence the transmission of hereditary factors in order to promote what is good and to eliminate what is harmful: this fundamental tendency is irreproachable from the moral point of view.' Not surprisingly he went on to query some of the more outlandish expressions of this aim of genetics and eugenics, and he particularly reacted against some of the means being advocated to further it, including abortion, eugenic sterilisation, AI etc. He went on to condemn the practice of genetic counselling, considering it proper, and even in most cases obligatory, to warn and advise against having children when there was reason to believe they might be defective.

In 1979 the World Council of Churches made a number of recommendations at the Massachusetts Institute of Technology including:

- To help UN agencies set international guidelines for all recombinant DNA technology involving direct manipulation of the gene and thus determining what life may be.
- To initiate consultation with UN agencies on the grave ethical issues in human genetic engineering, meanwhile opposing genetic engineering on the human fertilised ovum for purposes other than genetic defects.

On 4 April 1997 twenty European countries signed the first international convention to control research into human genetic engineering and cloning. The Convention on Human Rights and Biomedicine signed in Oviedo, Spain, banned the use of genetic engineering techniques for anything other than medical purposes and effectively outlawed human cloning. One of the officials from the Council of Europe which had masterminded the convention stated: 'It stops people toying with the human genome to make sure, for example, that their descendants all have blonde hair and blue eyes.' The accord also specifically prohibited the production of human embryos exclusively for research purposes and prevented parents using *in vitro* fertilisation techniques to select the sex of their children. Moreover, it banned the commercial trade in human organs. Interestingly the German government refused to sign the accord, declaring that the convention was not strict enough. Clearly the traumas of the eugenics research of the Third Reich are not easily forgotten. While the convention created a basic agreement on the limits of biomedical research across Europe it did not preclude individual countries from passing stricter domestic legislation.

According to Daniel Tarschys, the Council's Swedish Secretary-General, the convention established the principle that the interests and welfare of a human being should prevail over those of society or science. This led the convention to insert a strict declaration on a patient's right to be fully informed on the consequences of any medical intervention and to refuse that treatment. It also protects individuals from being discriminated against on the basis of their genetic make-up.

While the convention provides a number of worthy recommendations the main problem is that European biomedical companies can easily bypass its restrictions by carrying out experiments in majority world countries without legislation to control research. Clearly, while new laws in this area in developed countries are welcome, they are doomed to failure unless they are complemented by legislation in the majority world.

Conclusion

Johannes Reiter has studied the insights of various ethicists who have written about this issue and compiled what he sees as the 'ten commandments' to be applied to genetic engineering. These are not meant to be the last word on the subject but instead are guidelines to good practice in the field. They require to be reinterpreted on an ongoing basis and are intended to help ethical reflection among geneticists.

1. Interventions upon nature are ethically permitted and licit. They require a deep appreciation of the possible good and bad effects both for the present and for the future of nature and humanity.

2. The freedom of the researcher is not unlimited. Its boundaries are defined by the good of humankind. On the other hand, the risk of misuse ought not justify a moratorium on research.

3. Research should be conducted in an open manner. It ought not claim a monopoly of knowledge. There must be opportunities to reflect on and criticise the knowledge available.

4. Researchers alone carry responsibilities for their research, but share the responsibility for the possible application of their discoveries.

5. The aims of genetic engineering must essentially be oriented towards the therapeutic in the broadest sense. They are directed at a development of humanity and must make reference to criteria generally acceptable to the human community.

6. Boundaries must be set for genetic engineering. It ought not be a question of the domination of humankind by individuals. Research and the experimentation which it requires ought not pose a threat to life, health or the personal integrity of people, even before birth, nor put them in danger.

7. Once individuals are involved in genetic engineering, they must not be made only 'objects' and as 'means' pure and simple, of technical achievement; human dignity requires that they always be treated as subjects.

8. The genetic map or type should not be drawn up without the consent and for the good of the individual concerned and may not furnish the basis for any discrimination. The

fundamental rights of the person and the equality of humankind would thus be severely jeopardised.

9. To the extent to which it does not modify the psychosomatic (mental and physical) composition of humankind, genetic therapy is ethically justified. It imposes an awareness of the risks involved.

10. Having regarded to the principle of human dignity and to the right of individuals to their identity and their uniqueness, cloning is to be condemned unreservedly.[3]

One concept which has not yet entered into popular parlance is 'genetic pollution'. Let us hope it never does. Yet if genetic engineering is abused it could create a more insidious threat to humankind's survival than traditional environmental pollution. In the novel *The Boys from Brazil* rows of blue-eyed Aryans marched off assembly lines. This is not a likely scenario in the foreseeable future. Geneticists themselves have the same general objectives as doctors in the medical area: to reduce suffering, to increase the level of health and to increase the efficacy of new drugs. None the less it is not difficult to envisage a situation where some people will press for the right to apply genetic engineering to correcting inherited defects in adults, perhaps even in the unborn child. Our ability to sex an unborn child by looking at its genes might have major implications for the ratio of men to women, if the technique were to become widespread.

At its most extreme the most complete adoption of genetic engineering would require fundamental changes in the way we think about our place in the natural order. This could eventually lead the scientific community to decide upon a natural order, and to engineering nature according to our priorities at the time. In such circumstances the question would no longer be: Where does humanity belong in nature? Instead it would become: Has nature any place at all in an essentially artificial world? The likely consequences of such an arrogant attitude to biological conversation would be disastrous, both for biological conservation and for ourselves. Clearly genetic engineering will not allow us the luxury of learning by our mistakes, as we have done too often in the past.

At the moment it appears we have two realistic options. The option to sit back and hope for the best cannot be contemplated because keeping aloof ultimately involves complicity. On the one hand we can say a firm no to genetic engineering lest the worst horrors of the Brave New World strike us down. This involves turning our back on the possibilities for the advancement of humankind which it might offer us in terms of controlling our evolution, and the evolution of our animals and plants, for example research on the diminution of genetic disease. Cloning enables us to create plants tolerant to drought and so potentially turn deserts into fertile farmland. On the other hand we can accept the need for scientific freedom and the promise that genetic engineering offers us – mindful of the fact that it may have risks we cannot predict. However, such experimentation must be very carefully regulated, not just by the scientific community themselves, but by a well-resourced statutory body which would license such research and set strict guidelines.

6

DESIGNER GENES

Historically, the art of healing has always been the focus of ethical reflection. In ancient Greece, the Pythagoreans saw an intricate interrelationship between ethics, religion and health and the Jews often linked salvation and healing. The principle of therapy has always been seen as good. However, not all therapies are good. Some may not justify the expense or the unintended consequences. Genetic therapy raises particular ethical issues.

Etymologically, the word 'therapy' (from the Greek *therapeia*) originally meant 'service to God': later it meant 'service to human beings'. The human race, like all organisms, have a substantial genetic burden. We carry mutations in our DNA which are deleterious, or could be deleterious, in certain circumstances. This is the so-called 'genetic load'. It shows itself most dramatically when a child is born with a condition like haemophilia. One in fifty of all children is born with a serious genetic disorder. In Ireland this means that about one thousand such children are born a year.

Some people have an additional genetic load which predisposes them to certain conditions, for example we are all at risk of heart attack, but we differ in the genes that predispose us to heart attacks. In the late 1960s around a hundred genes which predispose us to cancer were discovered. Some of these have a dramatic and tragic effect and cause people to have a very high risk of cancer, for example a gene, recently identified, predisposes a small number of women to have breast cancer.

A gene for resistance to sleeping sickness in cattle has been developed and we can now transfer these genes effectively to cattle. Genes have also been developed for insect resistance. A former student of Trinity College, from Vietnam, has transferred the gene for insect resistance into cauliflowers and these cauliflowers appear resistant to butterflies. These advances hold out the prospect of great advances in agriculture. Likewise our knowledge of individual genetic disorders are rising very rapidly.

What constitutes a genetic liability? Illness is often more socially than medically determined, particularly mental illness. In the past, and even in the present, societies tended to deny freedom to dissenters and the 'abnormal' by discarding them in institutions rather than imprisoning them.

Skin colour has a significant genetic component. The old apartheid regime in South Africa was just one example of the way in which skin colour has formed a basis for segregation and discrimination. In such circumstances skin colour is a genetic liability. The correct ethical response to this situation is not genetic therapy but to break down the wall of prejudice that causes people to discriminate on the basis of skin colour.

Likewise, gender is often seen as a genetic liability; because of notions of male superiority some people in certain societies, like Chinese, do not want to have baby girls. Accordingly, sex determination is sometimes seen as genetic therapy. This is little short of nonsense because it assumes that gender is a form of illness.

The definition of human ailments depends largely on social situations – myopia could be a life-threatening liability in a remote jungle society, but is a mere inconvenience in our modern, developed world. Thus it makes much more sense to supply short-sighted people with glasses rather than resorting to expensive and risky genetic therapy.

Certain genetically influenced illnesses are stigmatised in various societies where they are particularly common: sickle-cell anaemia principally affects people of African origin; Tay-Sachs disease occurs largely amongst people of Ashkenazi Jewish ancestry; thalassemia major (Cooley's anaemia) is especially prevalent among people of Mediterranean origin and, as we have already seen, cystic fibrosis is most common among people of Northern European descent. Almost every identifiable group of people has in its gene pool certain troublesome characteristics. Humankind sometimes contributes to these problems by prejudice.

No gene is an island – genes do not operate in isolation. As we have seen already environmental and cultural conditions affect health. Genetic influences interact with environmental and cultural conditions to cause disease and it is often difficult to distinguish the part played by each. The environmental factors would include education, work and environment, unemployment, water and sanitation, health care services, housing, living and working conditions.

Non-inherited disease might be treated by replacing or repairing malfunctioning genes in a particular organ of the body. For example, a gene therapy treatment might at some point in the future be developed to treat a cancer. The treatment would involve altering genes in tissue in the affected organ so that they did not produce cancerous cells. Such intervention would not affect the hereditary material passed on by the patient in their egg or sperm. The germ line would remain unaffected. The diagnosis of a non-inherited disease might be improved by identifying mutant behaviour in the relevant genes.

Gene therapy

Bernard Hoose helpfully breaks down his analysis of the issue of genetic therapy into four headings: somatic cell gene therapy; germ-line gene therapy; enhancement genetic engineering; and eugenic genetic engineering.[1]

Somatic cell gene therapy relates to the attempt to correct the genetic defects in the body cells of the patient. Treatment of the reproductive cells is not involved. The first such trial began a few years ago on a little girl with a very rare immuno-deficiency disease which results from the absence of the gene responsible for the production of an enzyme known as adenosine deaminase (ADA). Normal ADA genes had been cloned in the laboratory. The plan was to get these genes into the white blood cells in the girl's body known as T lymphocytes, which form part of the immune system. To facilitate this the genes were inserted into murine (mouse) leukemia retroviruses which had first been made harmless. Some T lymphocytes were removed from the girl's body. The viruses then formed a transport system to carry the missing genes into the cells. The modified cells were then nurtured in culture and transfused into the girl's body.

Not surprisingly this case generated a series of ethical questions which had to be confronted before the trial could begin. What was the likelihood of causing cancer? What was the risk of the virus combining with other material in the girl's body to form a highly infectious virus? If both risks were negligible and the patient's condition was life-threatening and the possibility of benefit was very real such treatment could be considered to be ethically acceptable. Genetic therapy on somatic cells falls, broadly-speaking, into the same category as organ transplants – provided it does not change the human psychological structure.

Even when somatic cell gene therapy is successfully completed, the genetic defect could still be passed on to future generations. Germ-line therapy might be the solution to this problem, whereby the genetic correction would also need to be made in the reproductive cells of the patient. While this, in the words of Hamlet, is 'a consummation devoutly to be wished' there is a need for caution because any mistakes could be passed on to future generations. The future may bring advances in scientific knowledge which would remove such a risk but that is not now the case.

Cystic fibrosis is the most common hereditary disorder among white people. People with this condition are forced to undergo daily treatment to clear sticky mucus from their lungs, and most die in their twenties. Gene therapies are currently being tested on individuals suffering from a variety of conditions including CF. While sufferers will not benefit directly from gene therapy their children would be protected from inherited disease.

The initial attempt by a university in the US to patent a technique for germ-line therapy in humans shocked public opinion and was dismissed as premature. Even if such techniques are shown to be safe and reliable, it remains to be seen if they will be permitted. Abbey Meyers, president of the US National Organization for Rare Disorders remarked: 'If you'd put these techniques in the hands of physicians who worked for Adolf Hitler, you can imagine what would have happened.'

It is also argued that germ-line therapy would generate a proliferation of adverse biological and social effects, such as reducing the size of the human gene pool, or encouraging a 'black market' in therapy. Archbishop John Habgood of York encapsulated this view: 'People who are less than perfect would be steadily more disadvantaged, and this would tend to push people further into the realm of the unacceptable.'

Habgood is particularly troubled that germ-line therapy could lead to a consumerist approach to human qualities. In a radio interview he remarked that in a free market society if such a service is available there will be a temptation to offer it:

> I think you have to blow the whistle against the increasing tendency to treat humans as if they were assemblages of parts, the mechanisation of life, if you like…. The closer we move to what the human identity is, the more dangerous the ethical ground…. There's a mystery about being a human that we must not violate too much, and I think it's doing something fundamentally destructive to our understanding of ourselves.

Against that it must be recognised that changing genes in sperm or eggs could free future generations from inherited disease.[2] In certain cases germ-line therapy may be the only technology that offers hope for their children, for example where somatic-cell therapy would fail to benefit a newborn baby with a genetic disorder such as Tay-Sachs disease. In these circumstances the child's nervous system deteriorates rapidly, leading to early death, and it is unlikely that somatic-cell therapy would reach all the affected brain cells.

The influential British philosopher Baroness Mary Warnock has argued that parents are always making decisions that involve risks on behalf of their children, such as choosing to have them vaccinated. Deciding to have germ-line therapy is just a variation of this choice. Genetic therapy on somatic cells falls broadly into the same category as organ transplants – provided it does not change the human psychological makeup.

There are wider questions. If germ-line therapy is demonstrated to be successful in extreme cases, there would be pressure for it to be used in less extreme conditions. What should the cut-off point be? Should we restrict it to the treatment of lethal diseases? Should we allow it for conditions that are life-threatening but painful, such as arthritis? However severe the condition, if it is hereditary, germ-line therapy may be able to eradicate it. For a common disorder such an effort would be a huge initiative. But if it is possible, would we be wise to try?

Another consideration is that some disease genes also carry benefits. Sickle cell anaemia develops in people who have two copies of the gene. However, a single copy can protect the carrier against malaria. Eradicating genes before their role is understood could leave generations with a debilitating and unforeseen inheritance.

Another factor which needs to be considered is that germ-line therapy will inevitably be risky and mistakes are likely to be irreversible. Hence this procedure should not be resorted to lightly. Moreover, unforeseeable side-effects, particularly in psychological terms, might occur from fairly straightforward genetic procedures, such as replacing a defective gene with a healthy one. The problems are exacerbated by the fact that long-term psychological effects may not be detected in animal tests.[3]

It is interesting to note that few government reports tend to focus on somatic cell gene therapy rather than germ-line therapy itself. An example of this trend is the 1992 Clothier Report of the British Committee on the Ethics of Gene Therapy which stated that 'because little is known about the possible consequences and hazards, and any harm to future generations would take a long time to discover and deal with, this application of gene therapy needs to be considered quite separately from somatic cell gene therapy'.

In an article in the spring 1992 issue of *Science and Public Affairs* Baroness Warnock appears to accept the possibility of germ-line therapy not simply to cure disease but as a means to enhance normal characteristics. She argues that if it became possible to eradicate for ever immune deficiency, especially AIDS, by means of germ-line therapy, it would have to considered very seriously. In addition she stated that she did not wish to rule out forever the ethical acceptability of germ-line genetic manipulation at the embryonic stage.

Proponents of germ-line therapy say it offers a true cure of the many genetic diseases prevalent in the human population.

Moreover, by preventing the transmission of diseased genes, germ-line therapy would eliminate the need to perform costly and sometimes risky somatic cell gene therapy in multiple generations. Opponents would counter-argue that it would involve too many unpredictable long-term risks to the transformed subjects and their offspring to be justified. They also highlight the problem of consent of future generations as a factor which must be given serious consideration. This is a particularly pertinent point as germ-line therapy experiments would involve research with early human embryos that would have an impact on their offspring, in effect casting many successive generations in the role of non-consenting research subjects.

There is also an allocative dimension to be factored into the equation. Germ-line therapy techniques are unlikely ever to be sufficiently cost-effective to merit high social priority in the face of alternative approaches to the problem. Against this background the question of the integrity of genetic patrimony ought not be forgotten. Germ-line gene therapy techniques would violate the rights of subsequent generations to inherit a genetic endowment that has not been intentionally modified.

Ruth Chadwick argues that the engineering of human cells, both somatic and germ line (which affects subsequent generations' genetic make-up) are ethically acceptable if used to prevent or cure disease but not to enhance human qualities.[4] Unforeseeable side-effects might result from replacing a defective gene with a healthy one. Some effects, such as central nervous system deficits might not show up for years, may not have been predictable from animal studies, but we would be stuck with it. Detecting psychological side effects could prove to be very difficult. It is crucial that the possibility of causing psychological confusion or distress in those who will be born as a consequence of using these techniques be adequately addressed.

Enhancement genetic engineering is concerned with inserting

genes designed for improvement into a normal healthy person. In 1985, one of the world's leading geneticists, W. French Anderson, claimed that too little was known to be able to understand the effects of trying to alter the genetic machinery of a human being. He cites the example of some Americans who give growth hormone to their normal sons in order to produce very large football or basketball players:

> 'But even worse, why would anyone want to insert a growth hormone gene into a small child? Once it is in, there is no way to get it back out. The child's reflexes, coordination, and balance might all be grossly affected. In addition, even more serious questions can be asked: might one alter the regulatory pathways of cells, inadvertently affecting cell division or other properties? In short, we know too little about the human body to chance inserting a gene designed for "improvement" into a normal healthy person.'[5]

Another question which must be raised is whether or not enhancement engineering can be considered therapy or not. Eugenic genetic screening is the attempt to make improvements in a race by selection of the best specimens for breeding. Richard McCormick has no doubts about the ethics, or more accurately the lack of ethics, of this approach:

> 'It involves the attempt to intervene genetically to select for character traits, intelligence, various talents and mental and emotional characteristics. Specifically, such proposals are sheer fantasy because the traits in question are probably influenced by many unknown genetic factors. Furthermore, such genetic backgrounds interact with the environment in as yet very mysterious ways. Ethically, the matter is quite straightforward, and it is all bad. What characteristics are to be maximised to

get a "better" human being? Is brighter necessarily better? Or, more pointedly, is white skin preferable to yellow or black? and who decides all of this? Questions like this point inevitably to the wisdom of C.S. Lewis's assertion: "The power of man to make himself what he pleases means, as we have seen, the power of some men to make other men what they please".[6]

If the label fits

In November 1994, a researcher from an American university announced that he was returning his federal grant money to protest against potential germ-line engineering misuses of his research findings, as well as the findings of other researchers. A storm of controversy was generated the previous year when it was disclosed that scientists at George Washington University in the United States had cloned human embryos. Essentially, the technique involved 'splitting' an embryo into identical twins, triplets or quads. The scientists were apparently prompted by a desire to increase the chances of pregnancy resulting from IVF. An immediate problem presents itself: what is to be done with unused or defective embryos? More alarmingly, does this technique enable prospective parents to choose a frozen embryo on the grounds that it is genetically identical to a child that they have seen? Some commentators went so far as to talk of 'an embryo supermarket' and pointed out that a woman could give birth to her own twin.

In some respects the questions raised by this development are parallelled by the ethical issues in using the eggs of aborted foetuses to help infertile women.

Opponents of genetic manipulation often use the phrase 'playing God'. It is as if to simply use the phrase suggests that the activity is already shown to be demonstrably evil. Stripping away the emotion the phrase 'playing God' merits closer scrutiny. One could legitimately counter-argue that all of medical science is about playing God since its purpose is to improve people's physical and mental condition. If we consider interference in nature to improve our lot generally, we could argue that a very large percentage of all human activity can be classified as 'playing God'. Yet such activity is not in itself unacceptable ethical behaviour. My point is to show that we require a more adequate criterion than 'playing God' to establish whether or not a particular use of our creative capacities can be considered ethically unacceptable.

Gender-selection, whether brought about by means of genetic manipulation or by aborting foetuses of the undesired gender, deserves serious consideration because of its effects on the as yet unborn. In some parts of the world where there is a marked preference for male children, for example India, where four out of five births in some states are female, and, because of infanticide and selective abortion, there is an overall deficit of Indian females equivalent to the whole British female population, there could be considerable imbalance between the sexes as a consequence of such interference. However, there may be a case for gender-selection – though not on the enormous scale that cultural preference for male children might produce in some countries. There are some genetic disease which are gender-related because they are caused by genetic defects in the X chromosome. Women usually have two X chromosomes, one from each parent, whereas men have only one.

Problems arise when a defective, usually recessive, gene appears on the X chromosome. When passed to a boy from his mother (fathers can only give Y chromosomes to their sons), there is not a second X chromosome with a normal gene to counterbalance his problematic X-linked one. Consequently the boy is affected by an X-linked genetic disorder. However, a girl has another X chromosome, with a dominant, 'healthy' gene, and is consequently immune to this condition. She can, though, be a carrier. Diseases like haemophilia and muscular dystrophy can be extremely distressing and, accordingly, some parents-to-be might decide on an abortion if tests established that a male foetus was carrying the gene responsible for such a disease. An ethical evaluation of such a strategy would of course have to consider the question of abortion but perhaps in the future geneticists will discover ways of selecting the gender of children without recourse to abortion.

Conclusion

Genetic therapy is likely to be a process of last resort for exceptionally serious conditions that cannot be adequately treated by other methods. Although genetic manipulation might bring wonderful advances for humankind it may also bring unplanned risks. Given the complexity of genetic therapy, human experiments are fraught with risk. Even its 'successes' may generate side-effects that cause harm. One of the difficulties of the discussion is that the advantages to the individual and to the community are not always the same. The obvious question which arises is: what risks are justifiable for the sake of possibly great gains? Accordingly, some researchers have challenged the so-called golden rule of medical ethics, 'First do no harm'. Instead they argue for an adaptation of the phrase on the lines of: 'Be willing to do some harm that greater good may come.' However, despite the apparent attractiveness of this approach, particularly in terms of keeping costs to a minimum, it effectively allows people to be treated as means to an end. On the other hand it should also be recognised that if genetic therapy is successful it may also bridge the gap between the person and the community. When therapy, for example, moves from the point of healing diabetes to the point of correcting the genetic causes of diabetes, the result benefits both individuals and humankind generally.

Since genetic therapy offers humankind a major enhancement of its powers two questions which must be faced are: Who shall use this power and for what purposes? Who will regulate them? An ethical assessment of genetic therapy will reflect on the social context in which it is used, upon the ethical sensitivity of those with the power to use it, and upon the values for which it is used. Historically we have paid a high and unexpected social cost for scientific progress, e.g. the destruction of the ozone layer, pollution of various kinds and the destruction of many species. Since therapy is a good, there ought not be a hasty ethical judgment against it. Final judgment on the usefulness of gene therapy must be suspended. There remains a lot to be learned.

7

NE'ER THE TWAIN SHALL MEET?
CHRISTIAN ETHICS AND GENETICS

He had it all: a magnificent intellect; a hypnotic charisma and a striking appearance. Charles Raven was considered to be the foremost preacher in the Church of England in the first half of this century. Yet he never became a bishop because his theological opinions were out of step with those of most of his peers. As a result it was often said that he was the living proof that ability was the greatest impediment to advancement in the Church! His personality did not always work to his advantage: he was highly strung, quick to take offence, over-sensitive and didn't suffer fools gladly. In fact it was probably more accurate to say he didn't suffer fools at all.

He was born in London in 1885, the son of a barrister. Although he was born in the city he developed a passion for the study of nature at an early age. In those days there was little emphasis on science in public schools, so it was not until he attended university at Cambridge that he had the opportunity to pursue his interests. While he read classics and theology he was also allowed to listen to lectures on biology and to carry out experiments in laboratories.

He won a double first at Cambridge, but rather than continuing in academic life he initially opted for a job with Liverpool City Council before deciding to enter the ministry. In 1910 he married his first wife, and their four children were born between 1912 and 1918. During the First World War he became a chaplain; he was shelled and gassed, and was extremely fortunate to survive. These experiences had a profound impact on him and steered him towards a concept of God as 'the Creator Spirit' (the title of one of his most famous books) constantly at work in the world through a process of evolution which involves suffering and struggle.

In 1932 Raven returned to Cambridge as Professor of Divinity. Despite his expertise in the tradition of the early Church he often poked fun at some of its idiosyncrasies and once quoted with a wry smile the 1820 Trust Deed of a Kent non-conformist chapel which read: 'In no circumstances shall a priest who wears trousers ever be allowed to occupy a pulpit.' As the storm clouds gathered throughout Europe in the 1930s and a tidal wave of nationalistic fervour swept through Britain Raven did himself no favours in the popularity stakes by publicly advocating pacifism. He was a man far ahead of his time who argued for the ordination of women, which was one of the main reasons why he never became a bishop.

So why raise his name in a discussion of genetics? His particular concern was to show the complementarity between science and religion. He was a persistent champion of the 'life sciences' and the biological models which could be used to illustrate his belief in integration and unity. His theology was optimistic and evolutionary, and he felt strongly that science and religion should never have become alienated. By approaching the subject historically he believed that he would show the folly of separating the two worlds. I wish to defend the view that his approach has much to offer Christian ethics today.

It would be fair to say that the Christian Churches have reacted cautiously, even nervously, to the genetics revolution. The Catechism of the Cathlic Church, for instance, claims that efforts 'to influence chromosomic or genetic inheritance are not therapeutic but are aimed at producing human beings selected according to sex or other predetermined qualities. Such manipulations are contrary to the personal dignity of the human being and his integrity and identity which are unique and unrepeatable.'[1] Pope John Paul II warned in *Veritatis splendor* against tinkering with humanity and human testing.

However, there have been more positive strands to Christian reflection in this area. In 1982 the World Council of Churches issued a document called *Manipulating Life*. While the document has a number of interesting things to say about genetics one of its most refreshing statements is that it is no longer practicable to depend on 'precedents from the past to provide answers to questions never asked in the past'.[2] The distinguished German theologian Bernard Häring went even further: 'My first reaction to the astonishing beginnings and development of brain research was not a warning against manipulation but an expression of awe and admiration for man's capacity to decipher gradually the language of the brain, the code of the neurons, and their message. Admiration is my first response to the findings of science in the field of genetics, where scientists have been able to decipher the language of the genes.'[3]

Not so different

David Smith, in his valuable addition to the canon of literature on medical ethics, *Life and Morality*, draws attention to the fact that a number of episcopal conferences have sought to address the dangers and positive advantages of genetics.[4] He points to the example of the US Bishops' Conference in their 1978 Pastoral Statement on Handicapped People, where they enunciate a number of principles and outline the responsibilities of the Church at three levels: parish, diocesan and national. In particular they point to Jesus' practical concern for the disabled and argue that the Church would be in breach of its duty if it failed to show similar concern for those with disabilities today. Of course many people have disabilities because of a genetic defect. The bishops point to the fact that lip-service is not enough:

> We must actively work to realise these rights in the fabric of modern society. Recognising that handicapped individuals have a claim to our respect because they are persons, because they share in the one redemption of Christ, and because they contribute to our society by their activity within it, the Church must become an advocate for and within them. It must work to increase the public's sensitivity toward the needs of handicapped people and support their rightful demand for justice. Moreover, individuals and organisations at every level within the Church should minister to handicapped persons by serving their personal and social needs.[5]

The new ethical issues about genetics raise questions about the adequacy of Christian theology's reflection on disability to date. With a few honourable exceptions, notably Stanley Hauerwas, Christian theologians have not given this important area the attention it deserves. Advances in genetic screening raise new problematic questions for parents-to-be: Can I impose this on my children? To what extent do I then share responsibility for their condition? In the future the pressure on parents to have the 'perfect child' is likely to increase. The idea that people are only healthy if they can function normally in society points to the exaggerated expectations many people have about health care. Is there a risk that in the future people with disabilities will be seen as having slipped 'through the net'? At the end of their lives will they be seen as having outstayed their welcome?

New technological applications do not, in and of themselves, cause ethical dilemmas. Rather they are the occasion for complex ethical dilemmas in the future. A particular area for concern is how Christianity is to grapple with the problems of resolving society's responsibility to future generations. This point is well made by Rachel Iredale:

> On the one hand, we should not be making changes to the genetic structure of individuals which will adversely affect their descendants. On the other, we should perhaps try to remove the genetic damage that we can remove and which, if left in place, may harm potential people. Thus, a conflict arises between the ethical principles of beneficence (to do good) for humanity today, and nonmaleficence (to do no harm) to future persons.[6]

Human life is problematic, in so far as life proceeds by decisions, which we take at a particular time. To become human involves more than merely reacting to stimuli; we are moulded by the fundamental values, principles and rules which take on life when we act in freedom, that is when we act in a particular way and give our personal allegiance to that choice. It is because we *can* shape our lives that questions arise about *how* we should do so.

The capacity for shaping our life by choice and freedom is central to our development. It is also at the core of ethical decision-making. In many cases ethical choices do not occur in conditions where right and wrong are apparent, but rather the best decision must be wrested from less than ideal alternatives. In no field of human activity is this more apparent than in genetics.

Genetic science has extraordinary powers. These powers bring awesome responsibilities. On what basis does the ethicist claim to pass judgment on matters relating to genetics? Ethics extends to the whole of life and so there can be no legitimate compartmentalisation of the ethical and medical or genetic spheres.

For their part, Christian theology and ethics have also started to seek out the insights of other disciplines. The task of Christian theology is to interpret the meaning of the Christian experience with the God of Jesus Christ for us today and for our lives in this world. What has God's revelation in Jesus Christ's life, death and resurrection to say for us today? Christian theology understands the world as God's creation, as the place where God solicits human partners to participate in a covenantal relationship with a divine partner. This understanding compels Christians to work closely with all people of good will for the creation of a more just and peaceful world and also to discuss the composition of such a world with all interested parties. Consequently, Christians are challenged to take an active interest in all important activities such as politics, ecology, economics, culture, education and genetics. Christians may have a valuable contribution to make to these activities because of their particular understanding of God's presence in the world and of God's will for the world. Accordingly, it is appropriate to consider the insights of Christian theology in a discussion of ethical issues in genetics.

Christian ethics today is faced with a situation where pluralism and ambiguity are to the forefront. Ethics is characterised by uncertainty because all ethical claims have to be tentative since there are so many conflicting analyses of each question. Accordingly we need to submit our ethical presuppositions to fresh scrutiny on an ongoing basis and ceaselessly seek new and better answers for old questions as well as attempting to find answers for emerging questions. In such a situation talk of Christian ethics becomes problematic. As we have seen Christian ethicists have offered a number of different approaches to respond to the new situation in genetics. Most of their theories have valuable insights to offer but no system has all the answers. However, this discourse has tended to concentrate on the specific issues which are problematic at a particular moment rather than offering a coherent conceptual framework in which these difficulties can be discussed.

For this reason I wish to argue for a retrieval of the importance of the natural law in ethical analysis. Such a retrieval requires a critical re-interpretation of the natural law which appreciates the variety of the human situation; safeguards a legitimate place for exceptions and reflects the historical character of human nature.

A theological problem immediately presents itself. How can the natural law, being by definition secular, help to portray the realities of the Christian life? In the Christian perspective all people are creatures of God. Our nature is therefore determined by our createdness. The ethical imperative of nature is grounded, ultimately, in the metaphysical condition of the human person in the situation of salvation. Life is a vocation, a call to seek God. The manual tradition of Roman Catholic moral theology spoke of the 'taking up' of the natural law into Christianity. I wish to argue that the natural law is more correctly understood as an excision from Christianity, that is, it is in itself partial grace. The mystery of grace is a reality which pervades all of our creaturely life. If we talk of the natural law it must, therefore, be in the context of an understanding of nature and of grace which allows us to keep these perspectives.

Back to basics

Historically the term 'natural law' has led to such confusion and misuse that the first temptation is to ignore it altogether. However, the alternatives: rationality, personality, human rights, etc. are likely to be just as bewildering. The origins of the natural law can be traced back at least to the fifth century BC. In the *Antigone* of Sophocles a distinction is made between the written laws of the state and the unwritten law, which has a higher ethical claim on us because of our common humanity. This distinction was related to the controversy about the status of ethical duties generally: Are ethical obligations derived from human nature or convention?

A more developed theory of natural law emerged with the development of Stoic ethics, and its belief in the principle that the good life consists in living in accordance with nature, where 'nature' includes not merely our human nature but the entire natural scheme of things in which human beings have their place. A still more refined notion of natural law emerged with Aristotle (384-322 BC). He claimed that ethical duties could be ascertained by reflection on human nature. His view of nature was essentially teleological: nature produces nothing without a purpose. The purpose of every object was to realise itself fully.

Aristotle's position was developed by Thomas Aquinas. He correctly pointed out that the growth of what is natural in the human person is the necessary preparation for the growth of the fullness of growth within this humanity. However, a theory of pure nature led in the long term to the positing of an order of pure nature: a useful theory ultimately became a strait-jacket from which ethics was unable to set itself completely free. Despite initial advantages, the ultimate disadvantages became more apparent as the theory outlived its usefulness – the stress on the independence of nature, with its attendant dualism, came more to the forefront. The mystery of grace was sentenced to a quite unnatural exile. This historical development led to a nature enclosed and complete in itself, to which the supernatural was an external addition.

Thomas worked on the assumption that people must discover their own nature, through the use of their reason in the experience of freedom. In the Thomistic vision law is the result of a complex and continuous dialectical process, where the validity of law for the present socio-cultural realities is gauged against the underlying truth of metaphysical nature. While law has a valid place within ethical formulation its place is subject to continual analysis. Much ethical reflection after Thomas shortcircuited this painstaking analysis.

In the not too distant past ethicists used the phrase *contra naturam*. But what is nature? With contemporary research into the complex worlds of hormones, gonads and chromosomes we are less sure of the term 'nature' today than we were fifty years ago. The definition of nature is crucial. Our nature is human nature and despite our growing knowledge and insights, human nature is a mystery.

Ethics needs an adequate analysis of the nature of the human person: adequate according to the demands of anthropology and ethical reflection as they exist today. The scientific task of Christian ethics (specifically helping people to answer the question how they can live their lives as God wants them to live it) remains the same, just as the nature of the human person retains a radical similarity despite cultural changes. However, it is no longer acceptable for ethicists to work from the discredited anthropological premises and models of nature-grace which we considered. Christian ethics is neither a matter of direct religious revelation, nor is it, on the other hand, totally independent of the religious aspects of the nature of the person. Thus the Thomistic view of the natural law helps to state more clearly the religious dimension of ethics as well as the ethical dimension of Christian faith.

A primary attraction of the Thomistic natural law theory for Christian ethics is that it shows how the absolute supremacy of a creator God is compatible with the reasonable freedom of the human person's own creative response to the will of a personal God. For Thomas ethics was essentially reasonable, in that reason and intelligence are the key elements in the speculative and practical levels of ethics. This theory, which has major significance for those involved in the ethics of genetics, works from the premise that the human person acts with a general end in view (that good be done) but it does not lay down an inflexible and static notion of the good. Good is to be done not 'simply' because God wills it: but one must do something good if one is to act intelligently at all. It seeks to reflect the real experience of human beings but it opposes an ethics which is 'abstract' or 'authoritarian'. It seeks to take consequences into account – the future results of our actions are as important as the past. Natural law is historical and mutable: it does not mean that everything will change but that change is a possibility in all but the essential elements of human nature. Ethical judgments are exercises in the use of proportionate reasoning.

The current debate on the specificity of Christian ethics appears to be suggesting that, so far as content is concerned, Christian belief has nothing original to contribute to human ethical reflection at its most sophisticated. The ten commandments, for example, are not words from heaven, but an early ethical, perhaps legal, code elaborated in a particular culture. The Jewish and Christian ratification of such teaching gives it an additional extrinsic authority for their followers, but it does not thereby isolate this teaching from its genesis in human ethical experience and reflection. Moreover, it does not exempt it from the inherent deficiencies in all human judgments and discourse, particularly in the area of generalisations.

St Thomas claimed that the ethical principles to be found in the Old Testament in general added nothing new to the natural law, or, to use his term, 'the law of nature'; and that the ethical content and vocabulary of the New Testament added very little to the Old. His assertion that the commandments of the decalogue were unchangeable proved very influential, particularly in the Roman Catholic tradition. However, what was virtually ignored was his qualifying remark: 'What is changeable is the application of the commandments to individual acts, and whether such an act is, or is not, homicide, or theft, or adultery.' This is a crucial point because it correctly states that the function of reason in ethics is never simply to apply general principles to individual situations. The reality of the situation may not correspond to the ethical concept contained in the general principles, or to the common ethical terminology which expresses this concept, and so considers, for example, 'homicide' or 'theft' as unacceptable in all possible circumstances. Such terms are not merely descriptive, they are also evaluative. This neglect of the Thomistic qualification has created a very unhelpful, even dangerous, situation. Returning to the example of ethics in health care, when terms such as 'euthanasia', 'sterilisation' and 'abortion' are used to identify a particular situation or action, an ethical judgment on that situation has already been formed. However, such automatic responses are redundant because the new questions require new answers rather than simply the reiteration of old answers to quite different questions.

In this perspective, rather than preconceived answers, the focus is on facts and reflection and on seeking further facts and reflecting on them, to evaluate not only their possibilities but also their limitations. The new answers which ethicists are searching for have no value unless they can be argued for, if not demonstrated beyond all reasonable doubt. This process of argumentation is not an optional extra – a way of justifying one's own convictions. More positively it helps to subject them to intense scrutiny. There must be a dialectic between insight and reason.

The value of the natural law tradition for our discussion on ethics in genetics is that it attempts to provide arguments for or against a particular teaching. At first glance this might appear to be a weakness given the vulnerability of reasoning and argumentation which we have already considered. However, I wish to argue that this is actually a strength. Although we may not arrive at all the 'right' answers, by giving reasons we must expect counter-reasons from those who favour a different position. Through this debate we may revise and improve, or perhaps even reject, our initial insight or have it authenticated and accepted by others.

However, there is a major caveat when speaking about St Thomas as a guide to the shape of ethical reflection today. As we have seen already ethical reflection today is characterised by ambiguity and pluralism. As we have also noted Thomas was sensitive to the ambiguities of ethical situations but he could not have foreseen the pluralistic context in which we live. For this reason it is important that Thomas' approach be complemented by a recognition that in the light of the ethical diversity and the proliferation of ethical languages in the world today, we must expect to encounter different ethical languages issuing from different communities. This new pluralistic environment is an opportunity for ethicists to learn from a broader range of insights than has been available heretofore. Accordingly, the only possible constructive response to this situation is for groups and individuals to engage in a process of ethical reflection in an interdisciplinary way. The contemporary relevance of St Thomas is that he shows that ethics is not a closed system but a conversation with others, a search for answers which can only be provisional.

This understanding of natural law is of great value to reflective people of all religious traditions and none who are seeking a way to approach ethical dilemmas. In the contemporary situation we can either follow the example of fundamentalist movements and adopt an ethical system which pretends to have an answer for every different ethical question, or we can enter into an ongoing and laborious discussion on ethical principles. The natural law, properly understood, with its emphasis on reasoning and the provisional nature of ethical discourse offers students of the ethics of genetics a valuable way of approaching ethical questions. In this perspective good can be done if we act intelligently. Moreover, it introduces a much needed dialectic into ethics in genetics between principles and problems, between insight and reason.

Accordingly, those grappling with the ethics of genetics are compelled to discard their preconceived ideas and to reflect on their answers and questions, mindful of their possibilities and limitations. They may not arrive with all the right answers, rather, they need to have a healthy scepticism for their own infallibility. By giving reasons for their decisions they can benefit from the counter-reasoning of those who advocate a different position. Through this dialogue they may revise and improve or reject their original insights. The natural law helps to safeguard the critical edge of ethics and offers a conversational model to the ethics of genetics where the focus is on finding better answers to old questions and new answers for emerging questions.

The recent controversies on genetics have highlighted a major gap in ethical reflection on health care, namely the lack of an adequate approach to ethical theory. As Aristotle perceptively observed ethical argument or 'proof' is a particularly subtle and sensitive form of argument which does not admit either of the method or of the certainty of the natural sciences. The controversies about genetics have also highlighted the need for a larger vision in which difficult ethical questions can be considered which provides convictions, attitudes, motivations and norms. While this vision does not provide answers to the hard questions it provides a standpoint, an orientation, a co-ordinating system, a compass.

If the Church is to be a prophetic presence today it must be immersed in the task of building a better world. Contemporary society displays a proliferation of many interests, individual, social, environmental and medical, each demanding a fair share of the world's scarce resources. Unfortunately there are not enough resources available to meet all those needs. There is no easy ethical blueprint to which society can refer to establish that all of its obligations have been justly discharged. It is important that the Church's voice is heard on these issues. However, its voice must be an informed one.

In the Gospel we find Jesus repeating over and over again the simple advice 'Watch and pray'. This was not merely a readiness for unexpected death. It is far wider than that. It is an admonition to be alert to the call of God in one's immediate situation. In discerning how it is to respond most effectively to God's call today the Church must confront a whole series of problematic issues. This calls for a 'learning Church' which is open to specialist insights. The 'genetics revolution' raises many difficult questions. If the Church is to speak out on this issue that it is vital that it be in possession of the wisdom of the experts in this area.

Conclusion

A dialogue between Christian ethics and genetics is potentially valuable since it may unravel not only what Christian ethics has to offer the ethics of genetics; but also, equally importantly, what genetics can offer the Christian faith. It is not the task of Christian ethics to lecture at genetics 'from above', but to collaborate closely with geneticists in the interest of the mutual enrichment of both. To their credit geneticists have already shown an awareness of some of the ethical issues which are arising: a recent International Congress of Genetics in Birmingham passed a motion that discrimination on the basis of genetics should be banned.

Christian ethics is challenged to attain a proper balance between the fullness of faith and the need for rigorous argument. Christianity is not primarily about ethics. To be a Christian means to accept a religious way of life, to allow the interpretation of life found in Christ Jesus to shape one's existence. This becomes the unifying thread for one's life, the context in which all else is seen. It is life's predominant consideration which relativises all else.

There is not a Christian approach to ethics in genetics *per se* in the sense that Christianity has additional insights above and beyond other religious or secular traditions. Rather, in the Christian perspective genetics assumes a new dimension and significance. While Christians recognise that ethics and genetics is independently important, that ethical questions about genetics arise and can be solved by those who have rejected or never heard of Christ, for Christians genetics is part of a larger canvas. It becomes a determining factor in their relationship with God, with Christ, and in their understanding of the human community.

The ethical questions become a series of religious questions: What do God and Christ want? How am I to respond to them correctly in my professional or personal circumstances? Answers to these questions must be painstakingly, perhaps painfully, deciphered from reflection on the Christian tradition, from a myriad scripture references in the areas of losing and finding one's life, taking up the cross, thinking of others before self, laying down one's one life and seeking not one's own rights but the rights of others. These are not precise directives but orientation points growing out of how we regard ourselves and our world in Christ.

The danger of ignorance and incompetence looms over any attempt to unravel the contribution Christian ethics can make to genetics. As I suggested in the first section of this chapter, this danger is considerably reduced if a dialogical approach is pursued, which regards the ethics of genetics and Christian ethics as partners in a collaborative enterprise. Christianity does not have a blueprint for ethical reflection on genetics. Its insights do not translate easily into ethical reflection on genetics. However, I have tried to show that it can, to some limited extent, extend the scientific community's current level of ethical reflection by helping it to clarify what is meant by authentically human action in its emphasis on vision, disposition, intention and virtues.

In 1982 Pope John Paul II offered one practical example of this possibility in an address to biological researchers. He claimed that as the whole human person, spirit and body, is the ultimate goal of scientific research, even if the immediate object of the sciences is the body with all its organs and tissues. He went on to argue that the human body is not independent of the spirit, in the same way the spirit is not independent of the body, as is shown by the deep unity and mutual connection that exist between one and the other. He stressed the importance of scientific research which promotes knowledge of the corporeal reality and activity for the life of the spirit.

This nuanced approach is in sharp contrast to some commentators who argue that in our pluralistic societies there is no common understanding of a moral vocabulary, and thus we have no means of meaningfully discussing, let alone resolving ethical dilemmas. However, the fact that the principles are prima facie ones means that they cannot be applied woodenly. Discernment in particular cases will always be required. The certainty which many crave in moral issues is seldom to be had.

8

WHERE DO WE GO FROM HERE?

According to Voltaire 'history is the sound of hob-nailed boots ascending the staircase and of silk slippers coming down'. Genetics has come a long way since Gregor Mendel developed theories about inheritance from his experiments in a Moravian monastery garden. Since 1953, when Francis Crick and James Watson worked out the structure of DNA, which carries our hereditary messages in the form of genes, there has been a spectacular progression in our understanding of genetics and we have elevated this science to a new plane. It has also led to a situation where we face ethical dilemmas which previous generations could not have envisaged.

Splitting heirs

In October 1993 an American fertility expert, Dr Jerry Hall, announced at a scientific meeting in Montreal that he had cloned human embryos. Splitting embryos, as Hall had accomplished, uncovered a technique that could give doctors the ability to produce identical twins, and possibly triplets or quadruplets or even more, to order. There was also speculation that one might keep a spare copy of oneself in deep freeze, to be grown to maturity later so that its organs might be 'cannibalised' as the need arose: new parts for old, and a perfect genetic match to ensure compatibility. Hall justified his discovery on the grounds that it could be helpful to infertile couples by increasing the number of laboratory-fertilised embryos available for transfer into the womb. As less than one in ten of such embryos 'take', a stock of spares could increase the success rate for pregnancies. The Vatican intervened immediately, describing the move as capable of leading humanity down a 'tunnel of madness', and demanded that such 'perverse' work be banned. It argued that the moral abyss into which approval of cloning would lead us brought closer the age of designer humans when parents would select carbon-copy embryos for super-intelligence or other qualities. Significantly, even before this controversy, the British Human Fertilisation and Embryology Authority had considered the ethics of human cloning, and come down firmly against it.

Jeremy Rifkin, the founder of a biotechnology watchdog group in Washington DC argued: 'We are at the point of being able to mass-produce human beings. That is no less important than the first time they split the atom.' One of the persistent disappointments of what sometimes passes for ethical discussion on genetics is that it generates more heat than light. Emotive statements replace carefully crafted, nuanced arguments which provide an adequate philosophical framework against which complex issues can be addressed in an informed way.

Hall's experiments with embryo cloning were preceded for several years in agriculture. Researchers select parent animals with certain desired characteristics, for example lean meat. They then put egg and sperm together, and 'multiply' the embryo in laboratory conditions into genetically identical copies.

Many animals have been cloned in this way without negative consequences. However, the experience of one US biotechnology company based in Houston, Texas, deserves careful scrutiny. It successfully impregnated about one thousand cows with cloned embryos before serious problems emerged. Some of the calves grew to double their normal birthweight, 150lb or more instead of the normal 80lb, and had to be delivered by caesarian section. It subsequently emerged that these calves had severely disordered metabolisms at birth, with abnormal levels of oxygen, insulin and glucose in their blood. They had to be treated like premature babies for several weeks. It appears that the abnormalities were the consequence of faulty development in the placenta, the life-support network through which an embryo receives its nourishment while in the womb. As soon as embryonic cells start to take on separate roles, one of their first functions is to establish the placenta, and cloning appears to have interrupted the process. This incident serves as a salutary reminder of the potential pitfalls facing pioneers in this field.

Frankenstein revisited

The genetics revolution has given a whole new meaning to the famous line from *Star Trek:* 'It's life, Jim, but not as we know it'. In January of this year Dr Richard Seed, a Chicago scientist, announced his plan to clone a human being within the next two years and that he had already assembled a team of doctors and childless couples for the experiment. Seed has a doctorate in physics and helped pioneer the first successful transfer of a human embryo from one woman to another in the 1970s. This decision flies in the face of a recommendation of the US National Bioethics Commission the previous year that legislation should be passed banning such cloning. The President also banned any provision of federal funding for research in this area.

However, Seed availed of a loophole in US law which permits human cloning backed by private funding. He claimed that he had raised several hundred thousand dollars but needed $2 million to begin the cloning project. He added that he had selected four couples from a pool of six that had volunteered to be cloned; preparations were 90 per cent complete and he said he would go to Mexico if prevented from carrying out his experiment in the US.

In the course of a radio interview Seed elaborated on his philosophical presuppositions: 'I've said many times that you can't stop science. God made man in his own image. God intended for man to become one with God... Cloning and the reprogramming of DNA is the first step to becoming one with God.'

Within a week officials from seventeen countries had gathered in Paris to sign the first agreement to ban human cloning. After President Clinton denounced his plans Dr Seed went even further in a television interview: 'I have been enormously encouraged in just one day by calls I have received from infertile couples who are in tears. They say things like, "Don't let them stop you". My target is to have a two-month pregnancy in a year-and-a-half. It's not a difficult project.'

Despite Dr Seed's history of applying animal reproductive techniques to humans his claim that cloning is not a difficult operation is startling. While the scientific principle behind the process is relatively straightforward, the process within the laboratory is much more problematic, for example it has not yet proved possible to clone mice. Dolly was only created on the 276th attempt. In all previous efforts the embryo had failed to survive.

Ironically, the creator of Dolly, Dr Ian Wilmut of the Roslin Institute, has already stated that human cloning would not be ethically acceptable. However, not all scientists nor even ethicists would fully agree. The American Society for Reproductive Medicine has found that research into the technique of embryo-splitting, a different form of cloning from that employed to generate Dolly, is ethically permissible given its potential benefit to infertile couples. Of course we should help infertile couples. There is a number of ethically acceptable ways of doing this, from IVF to adoption. However, to claim that the problems of infertile couples are so pressing that we have to rush into cloning, is unacceptable.

Significantly, on Friday, 13 February 1998, at the height of the Iraqi crisis, President Clinton took time out to address the 150th annual conference of the American Association for the Advancement of Science in Philadelphia. In the course of a wide-ranging address he pointed out that if science as a whole were deemed to be acting unethically, politicians would have no option but to introduce draconian controls on all sorts of scientific research.

The ethical issue of which the proponents of human cloning seem oblivious is its impact on the allocation of scarce resources. How could such an exotic and expensive procedure be justified for an elite few when so many millions throughout the world are denied basic health care and effectively condemned to premature deaths?

There are divergences of opinion on the possibilities raised by human cloning. I wish to defend the view that at this moment in time it cannot be rejected out of hand on purely instinctive terms. Rather it must be proved that it is ethically unacceptable, given the present levels of uncertainty and confusion attached to it. This rejection of human cloning will include a consideration of such far-reaching questions as when life begins, the role of genes in determining personality, and the relationship between mind and body.

Money, money, money

Another potential minefield is the commercial exploitation of genetic advances. In France in 1994 a controversy emerged involving one of the country's best known scientists, Daniel Cohen, over his dual role as director of a centre for genetic research (CEPH) in Paris and as a co-founder and shareholder of Millennium, a leading American biotechnology company. CEPH, which is part-funded by the state, had discussions with Millenium with a view to collaborating in a search for the genetic causes of diabetes and in the development of treatments. CEPH has a gene bank containing DNA samples from 5,500 diabetics and their families. Millennium asked CEPH for exclusive rights to the DNA samples in exchange for $400,000 a year and royalties on any treatment developed from research. However, the collaboration faced a severe setback when Philippe Froguel, the scientist who had built up the gene bank, went public about his opposition to the collaboration.

Although this incident poses many difficult ethical questions it has to be recognised that the sheer scale of biomedical research virtually guarantees that public funds alone are not sufficient. Inevitably there will be collaboration between researchers and industrialists. Again there is need for strict regulation to legislate for questions such as: Have researchers the right to make a profit from work they have undertaken in government-funded laboratories? Who owns the commercial rights to DNA samples people have donated? What restrictions, if any, are needed to regulate the circumstances in which commercial companies can put patents on gene sequences?

Ethicists cannot simply pontificate about genetics but must join geneticists and other interested parties as colleagues in a collaborative enterprise in a sustained and vigorous search for answers about the new questions which are emerging in this area. One of the big challenges facing parents-to-be and the medical profession will be how to assess their genetic risk. Every newborn baby in Ireland is routinely tested as part of a national screening programme for a variety of inborn errors of metabolism. For many deleterious conditions people may be tested in order to establish potential genetic diabilities, or those of their offspring, that may be amenable to treatment. This poses new difficulties for doctors hoping to secure informed consent from patients affected in this way.

Consenting adults

In a landmark decision in 1995 the Irish Supreme Court decided that doctors might cease feeding a woman, who had been in a coma for over twenty years in a Dublin institution. As a twenty-two-year-old she had suffered three cardiac arrests during a minor gynaecological operation, resulting in very serious brain damage. While the woman was not dependent upon an artificial respirator she was assisted in feeding by a tube which was inserted into her stomach.

One of the many interesting features of the Supreme Court's judgment in this so-called 'right to die' case was Ms Justice Denham's description of the communication between the medical profession and the family in the early stages of the tragedy as 'reminiscent of a Victorian era'. The other medical, ethical and legal issues have been trawled extensively. However, this aspect of the judgment has received neither the attention nor the response it deserves.

The judge's comments highlight the desirability of inculcating a new culture of information provision and questioning into all health service relationships. This, at a stroke, would transform the old paternalistic relationship between doctors who 'know best' and patients who are expected passively to accept the information and treatment they are given. It would enable a decision-making process to come into being which is considerably better informed at all levels and, to use the buzz phrase, 'transparent'.

Medical care is based not on certainties but on probabilities. Every diagnosis involves an element of risk, the chance of an unfavourable outcome for a patient. An adequate understanding of risk is crucial to giving a valid consent particularly as many medical treatments have potent interventions that have side effects which are unlikely to be free from hazard. The explanation of risk also has major implications for litigation in medical care.

The health care professional's job, which connects daily with the pains and fears of others, carries with it commitments which are not usual in most other jobs, or at least, not to the same degree. Patients, by virtue of their increased vulnerability, must entrust a greater part of themselves to the good will of their doctors. They hope, justifiably, for a response to that trust which treats them with human concern and respect, as well as with professional knowledge and skill. A recurring problem, though, is the conflict the doctor may experience between the requirements of benefiting the patient and simultaneously respecting the patient's autonomy. In some such conflicts paternalism may ensue. As Ms Justice Denham's comments indicate, a new culture of 'transparency' is required whereby patients, or their guardians, are provided with adequate information. A balance is required between potential good and potential harm. Often this balance can be difficult to summarise and explain to patients.

Doctors are faced with a double challenge: to develop their communicative skills and to retain their firm commitment to the welfare of the patient so as to empower patients, by enabling them to make informed choices. This is not to imply that doctors have to inform patients about every conceivable risk, however remote, in a particular course of treatment. A 'fully informed choice' may not be possible because doctors could not be expected to communicate every possible risk to a patient nor could patients be expected to understand all the complexities of all possible treatments. Equally, a 'fully informed choice' may not be desirable for all patients as unnecessary anxiety might be generated in some if they were informed about every possible risk.

Information is not an end in itself. It is only useful if it provides helpful answers to pertinent questions and empowers patients to make good decisions. How to frame questions about health care becomes a crunch issue. Indeed, for this reason, a number of commentators in the UK have advocated a series of 'catechisms', which people could resort to in a variety of circumstances. Given the historical baggage attached to the term 'catechism', the word 'protocol' might be more suitable in the Irish context.

The formulation of 'user-friendly' protocols which would assist both patients and professionals to become partners in the information exchange process. The protocols would outline some of the key questions patients would need to have answered before they could give a valid consent to treatment. How would such protocols work in practice? Let us suppose a patient is seriously ill and the doctor suggests a new treatment with drugs which carry the risk of side-effects. The protocol would outline the sort of questions a patient would need to ask before consenting to such treatment. The questions could include the following:

- What are the likely side-effects?
- What is the prognosis without this treatment?
- What is this treatment designed to accomplish?
- Are there alternative treatments?
- In what circumstances would treatment be altered or terminated?
- How much research has been carried out on this drug?
- Would the physician use the same treatment on her/himself or on loved ones?

Individual protocols would be drawn up for specific categories of patients, for example patients with genetic disorders such as cystic fibrosis; dental patients and dialysis patients. To enhance the transparency process it would also be helpful if a 'health care professionals' contract' was debated and published in which the health care professionals' obligations to patients, colleagues and society were clearly spelled out. This could well be in the professionals' own interests given the increase in litigation in health care. A significant statistic is that according to a recent study, in 90 per cent of cases litigation in health care is the result of inadequacies in the doctor's communication rather than incompetence.

In the Irish context such communication problems are almost inevitable. The president of the Irish Medical Organisation, Dr Hugh Bredin, has stated that doctors are being forced to communicate with their patients at bedsides in obsolete, Victorian-style wards, within earshot of other patients. Moreover, due to lack of facilities doctors often have to communicate with patients' relatives in corridors rather than in private rooms.

Independent ethics appeal boards might be established on a trial basis to deal with the conflicts which arise between doctors and patients or their families. Patients would then have their grievances dealt with in a much less combative and expensive forum than a court of law. The appeals board would comprise a broad range of representation, with medical, legal and ethical expertise and patient's representatives. The verdict would be binding on both sides. However, the priority ought to be to ensure that cases do need to go to arbitration in the first place. Better communication between doctors and patients would go a long way towards achieving this.

Geneticists will continue to identify more and more genes which cause susceptibility to disease. However, medicine may not fully understand all the purposes these genes may serve. The gene for sickle-cell anaemia, which causes havoc in West Africa, also confers some immunity against malaria. At the moment we don't know the full facts of these genetic networks of causation, nor do we have an ethical consensus on how best to deal with them. As Rachel Iredale points out:

> Overcoming geneticity (the irrational fear of genetics based on its past history and the strong emotions stirred by DNA research) should also be an important priority. The abuses of genetics and the sinister uses to which it was put in the past are

unlikely to be repeated with an educated and informed public. However, without the appropriate debates and discussions, it might be argued that we are at the risk of threatening our very humanity.[1]

This debate must be well argued, informative, all-embracing and a fair appraisal of the prospects for the future including the benefits which might accrue, while offering realistic safeguards and prohibitions. The Dutch have shown the way forward in terms of the type of reflection that is necessary. In 1989 the Health Council of the Netherlands produced a detailed 196-page report entitled: *Heredity: Science and Society: On the possibilities and Limits of Genetic Testing and Gene Therapy.* The report was drawn up by four geneticists, two experts in health law, two ethicists, and experts in philosophy, social medicine, medical information and toxicology. It is a carefully nuanced document which, on balance, encourages the application of new techniques but points out potential danger areas.

The committee considered genetic diagnosis and counselling, genetic registers, cell banks, population screening, pre-implantation testing, gene therapy, and genetic testing outside the health-care system with special reference to insurance and employment. It also considered related issues such as the social, ethical and legal implications and the possible effects for individuals and for society at large. The report strongly rejects mass screening *per se* as a goal. Particularly welcome is the recommendation that the use of genetic testing by insurance companies for prospective clients, and also the disclosure of prior genetic information should be banned. Likewise, it dismisses genetic testing in the selection process for employment, except in unusual circumstances when it is in the interests of a third party or to protect the health of the person. Not alone does the report stress that limits must be put on access to genetic information to preserve confidentiality, it also recommends that the use of any genetic data should be restricted to the purposes for which it was collected, and asks for monitoring committees to be established to ensure compliance in this matter.

In the interests of balance

Too much of our ethical discourse about genetics has been couched in vagueness. The genetics revolution is likely to lead to:

1. A much more efficient means of food production. The green revolution is a fruit of genetics. In the 1950s there were major food shortages in India but now that country is self-sufficient in rice and wheat due to genetic advances. Likewise there is now a huge surplus of rice in China thanks to new genetic strains.
2. A much better health care system.
3. Many fewer children will be born with serious genetic disorders.
4. We will obtain vast new knowledge about how human beings work and how they have changed over evolutionary time, for example new knowledge of the brain will be of great interest to philosophers and psychologists.

However, there are a number of important questions which give grounds for concern. I would like to offer some personal suggestions to attempt to charter the ethical agenda in genetics.

- There is a vital need for public discussion on all aspects of the genetics revolution given the gaps in public knowledge, not alone about genetics but about science in general. In 1988 a survey found that two-thirds of people questioned still thought that radioactive milk could be made safe by boiling. In this context the role of the media will be crucial. At its best the fourth estate will provide an invaluable public service by acting as a watchdog on poor quality services and eugenical tendencies. A danger, though, will arise if people are led to believe that 'miracle cures' are just around the corner. Equally there is a danger of sensationalism which raises groundless and non-existent spectres, and exploits people's fears unscrupulously.

- The establishment of a national interdisciplinary commission to examine the main issues raised by the 'genetics revolution' ought to be seriously considered. This commission would include geneticists, scientists, policy makers, health care professionals, ethicists, etc. It would have a wide brief to include such issues as the restrictions that might be needed on the patenting of parts of the human genome. There will also be difficult questions to be resolved about the allocation of expensive genetically engineered drugs for rare or common diseases. Who should be treated when not all can be treated? For example who should receive genetically engineered betaseron, which might be effective against multiple sclerosis?

- As we have seen, many people are anxious about the control that may result from the genome project. However, we must also be alert to the danger of the illusion of control, the belief that the mapping enterprise may lead to the view that people's problems are thought to be primarily genetic. The culs-de-sac of biological reductionism and determinism must be avoided.

- It is prudent to ask what problems genetic screening brings from a civil liberties point of view. One specific area of concern is discrimination. The most fundamental right of people, from a civil liberties perspective, is the right to be treated equally. Professor Peter Humphries of

Trinity College is a world authority on the genetics of blindness. He has been able to identify certain genes which can be detected in a person who is not blind, but who will go blind in the future. Will employers want prospective employees to be tested for such predispositions?

There could be a temptation for immigration authorities to produce information about a particular group's genetic make-up. One reason to be concerned in this regard is that people from disadvantaged backgrounds are more at risk from genetic discrimination. To take the example of America (which many people would consider as the cradle of democracy), before the Nazis got into the business of eugenics in the 1930s, eugenical philosophy was rampant in the US. People who were considered genetically inferior, Mexicans for example, were kept out of the country. There is certainly a danger that an ill-formed political or social sense could use genetics as a pretext to discriminate against people who are on social welfare or who are considered to use public health care to an excessive degree.

This could be seen as alarmist, but I wish to defend the view that occasionally sounding alarm bells is justified on the basis that it contributes to raising public awareness. To those who still argue that sounding the alarm bells is alarmist my answer is to look to the lessons of history. In the 1920s in America the Supreme Court upheld a law which provided for compulsory sterilisation when there were three generations of criminals in a family. This is a fundamental violation of human rights.

Testing for late-onset disorders such as Huntington's disease, and for genetic predispositions and susceptibilities will become ever more prevalent. Already blood banks and private sperm banks contain a wealth of genetic information – so much so that they might even be termed DNA databanks. Genetic tests are not in themselves objectionable; what may be objectionable are the uses to which they are put.

Although countries will draw up their own guidelines for the application of genetics there is need for an international response because there is a risk that one or more countries will step out of line. As we have seen, in India female embryos are being destroyed, which is a very significant manipulation of the gene pool. To date the international community has shown very little concern about this. It is the responsibility of the state to ensure that all science and technology is carried out correctly. Genetics fits into that framework.

Many people do not wanted to be tested, as they don't want to know about their genetic susceptibility to a particular condition. Health care professionals will be challenged to prepare for the unpredictability of patients' responses to genetic tests. In some circumstances a positive test could be the catalyst for a deterioration in health.

The genetics revolution has given a new impetus to the nature versus nurture debate. An excessive emphasis on genetics could lead people to think genetics is reponsible for 'causing' disease and, equally, for averting it. Yet the cause of disease is multifactorial, and therefore to focus tightly on genetics we frame the relationship between health and responsibility too narrowly, excluding other questions that might also be relevant. This juxtaposition of the language of health and the language of genetics raises an important issue: is the aim of genetic medicine to relieve pain and suffering, or to transform the human condition – to care or to cure? As the mysteries of the genome become known to us will the new genetics pave the way for a definition of health in terms of the optimal functioning of the human person? Does that mean that we pursue every possible genetic therapy? Significantly, in the UK the Nuffield Council on Bioethics has called on the Government to set up a 'central co-ordinating body' to oversee genetic testing and to monitor how it is to be implemented in the National Health Service, industry and the workplace, and goes on to warn of the threat of social stigma and abuse that could result from widespread genetic screening.

While testing offers many desirable possibilities there has to be adequate regulation in which quality is maintained. Those offering genetic tests commercially should be held accountable for the possible adverse effects of testing without facilities for counselling and follow-up. Another question to be confronted is whether it is ethically acceptable to devote more and more resources to the detection of rarer and rarer conditions. Particular care must be given to the issue of gene testing by post. The chief problem with this practice is that information is supplied to patients without putting the counselling back-up in place to prepare the patient to receive the information. The potential for a genetic disorder to disturb family relationships must also be recognised.

Genetic screening of workers should not take place at the expense of solutions to other problems, for example a concern to rid the workplace of hazardous chemicals should not be superseded by an attempt to screen workers with vulnerable genes.

While genetic screening does offer benefits there is a danger that some people may be over-enthusiastic in their own efforts to persuade people to participate in genetic tests. As we have seen in previous chapters the diagnostic and predictive potential of genetic knowledge has created problems in both the clinic and the workplace that cannot be ignored. What are we to do with genetic conditions that will only be expressed in certain environments? How do we deal with diagnostic genetic techniques that yield highly inaccurate and probabilist information about conditions whose onset may be many years away?

Advances in prenatal diagnosis of genetic defects will raise fresh questions about procedures like amniocentesis, in which some of the amniotic fluid in the sac surrounding the foetus is removed and cultured. Although amniocentesis screening is routinely available for women over thirty-five in the UK and the US that is not the case in Ireland.

It must also be remembered that one group of the population who deserve special consideration are the adopted, who may not have any genetic history on record.

Conclusion

The forthcoming explosion in genetics can be the story of a prism or a prison. It is time we woke up to the enormity of the changes that await us. This book is intended to help public discussion on these important questions. Rather than waiting for problems to arise and resorting to crisis management it would be more constructive to have adequate safeguards in place to ensure that people's integrity will not be trampled on. As any doctor will tell you prevention is better than cure. We cannot let the ethical questions in genetics be settled by default.

NOTES

Chapter 1: If it's DNA it's OJ

1. For a fuller discussion of the issues dealt with in this section see Averil Brown et al., 'The Green Revolution ... and now the Gene Revolution', *The Irish Scientist,* September 1994, 17.
2. Steve Jones, *In the Blood: God, Genes and Destiny* (London: HarperCollins, 1996) 75-6.
3. Ibid., 64-5.
4. Ibid., 64.
5. Francis Crick, *The Astonishing Hypothesis* (London: Simon and Schuster, 1994), 64.
6. For a fuller development of these issues see the Welsh Health Planning Forum's *Genomics* (1995).
7. London: Fourth Estate, 1996.

Chapter 2: Genesis Revisited

1. My debt to Steve Jones' book *The Language of Genes* in this chapter will be evident to all who are familiar with his work.
2. Thomas Henry Huxley, *In Defence of Darwin,* pamphlet, 1863.
3. W. S. Gilbert, *Understanding History* (London: London University Press, 1865), 74.

4. Steve Jones, op. cit., 9.
5. Ruth Hubbard and Elijah Wadd, 'The Eugenics of Normalcy', *The Ecologist*, Vol 23, No. 5, Sept/Oct 1993, 188.
6. B. Glass, 'Science: Endless Horizons or Golden Age?', *Science*, Vol 171, pp. 22-9.

Chapter 3: After the Brave New World

1. Cf. Walter Bodmer and Robin McKie *The Book of Man: The Quest to Discover Our Genetic Heritage* (London: Little, Brown, 1994).
2. Andrea Bonnicksen, 'Genetic Diagnosis of Human Embryos' *Hastings Center Report*, July-August 1992, S1.
3. Steve Jones, *The Language of Genes* (London: Flamingo, 1993), 3-4.
4. US Congress, Office of Technology Assessment, *Mapping Our Genes* (Washington DC: Government Printing Office, 1988), 84.
5. Jones, op. cit., 294.
6. Ibid.
7. Ruth Hubbard and Elijah Wadd, 'The Eugenics of Normalcy', *The Ecologist*, Vol 23, No. 5, Sept/Oct 1993, 185.
8. R.C. Lewontin, *Biology as Ideology* (New York: Harper Perennial, 1993), 68.
9. Ibid., 66-7.
10. A. Lippman, 'Commentary' *Hastings-Center Report*, July-August 1992, S20.
11. A. Lippman, & P. L. Bereano, 'Genetic Engineering: Cause for Caution', *The Globe and Mail*, 25 June 1993.
12. Lewontin, op. cit., 67.
13. E. Fox Keller, 'Nature, Nuture and the Human Genome Project', in D.J. Kevles & L.Hood, *The Code of Codes* (Cambridge: Harvard University Press, 1993), 281.
14. D. Nelkin and L. Tancredi, 'Classify and Control: Genetic

Information in the Schools', *American Journal of Law and Medicine,* Vol. 17, 1991, 67.

15. D.E. Koshland, 'The Future of Biological Research: What is possible and what is ethical', *MBL Science,* Vol. 3, 1988-9, 10-15.

16. Ruth Hubbard and Elijah Wadd, op. cit., 185.

17. S. P. Helmrich, 'Physical activity and Reduced Occurrence of Non-Insulin-Dependent Diabetes Mellitus', *New England Journal of Medicine,* Vol 235, 1991, 542-7

18. Hubbard and Wadd, op. cit., 185.

Chapter 4: The Genetic Detectives
References

1. Steve Jones, *The Language of Genes* (London: Flamingo, 1993), 66.

2. Kathleen Nolan 'First Fruits: Genetic Screening', *Hastings Center Report,* 1992, S2.

3. Ibid., S4.

4. Andrea Bonnicksen, *Hastings Center Report,* 1992, S10.

5. Ibid.

Note: For a comprehensive overview of the ethical issues involved in genetic screening see *The Danish Council of Ethics Annual Report,* 1992.

Chapter 5: The Eyes Have It

1. John Carey (ed), *The Faber Book of Science,* (London: Faber & Faber, 1995)

2. John Mahoney, 'The Future of Man', *The Month,* (September 1979), 278

3. Johannes Reiter, *Ethische Implikationen der Gen. Forschung Stimmen der Zeit* (July 1984), 435-447.

Chapter 6: Designer Genes

1. Bernard Hoose, 'Theological Trends', *The Way,* January 1995, 55-61.
2. James V. Neel, 'Germ-line gene therapy: another view', *Human Gene Therapy 4* (1993), 128.
3. Andy Coghlan, 'Hidden costs of a clean inheritance', *New Scientist,* 14 May 1994, 14-5.
4. Ruth Chadwick (ed.), *Ethics, Reproduction and Genetic Control* (London: Routledge, 1987).
5. W. French Anderson, 'Human gene therapy: scientific and ethical considerations', *The Journal of Medicine and Philosophy* 10 (1985), 288.
6. Richard A. McCormick, *The critical calling: reflections on moral dilemmas since Vatican II* (Washington DC: Georgetown University Press, 1989), 266-7.

Chapter 7: Ne'er the Twain Shall Meet

1. *The Catechism of the Catholic Church* (Dublin: Veritas, 1994), 2274.
2. *Manipulating Life: Ethical Issues in Genetic Engineering* (Geneva: World Council of Churches, 1982), 11.
3. Bernard Haring Manipulation (Slough: St Paul Publications), 1975 p.159
4. David Smith, *Life and Morality* (Dublin: Gill & Macmillan 1995), 165-6.
5. National Conference of Catholic Bishops of US, *Catholic Bishops on Handicapped People* (Washington, DC: United States Catholic Conference, 1978), 3.
6. Rachel Iredale, 'The age of the gene?', John Scally (ed.), *Ethics in Crisis?* (Dublin: Veritas, 1997), 87.

Chapter 8: Where Do We Go From Here?

1. Rachel Iredale, 'The age of the gene?', John Scally (ed.), *Ethics in Crisis?* (Dublin: Veritas, 1997), 89.

SELECT BIBLIOGRAPHY

Emmanuel Aglus, 'Germ-line Cells: Our responsibilities for future Generations', *Concilium,* 1990, 105-115.

W. French Anderson, 'Prospects for Human Gene Therapy' *Science,* 1984, 401-409.

Bioethics, vol. 5, no 3, 1991 – special issue: 'The Human Genome Project: where will the map lead us?' The issue comprises three articles:

1. Darryl Macer, 'Whose Genome Project?' 183-211.
2. Dorthy C. Sertz & John C. Fletcher, 'Privacy and Disclosure in Medical Genetics examined in Ethics of Care', 212-232.
3. Loane Skene, 'Mapping the human genome: Some thoughts for those who say "There should be a law on it" ', 233-249.

Edouard Boné, 'Genetic Engineering: How far may we go?' *The Month,* November 1986, 288-295.

Philip Elmer-Dewitt,'Cloning: Where Do We Draw the Line?' *Time,* 8 November 1993, 63-68.

Raanan Gillon, 'Ethics of Genetic Screening' *Journal of Medical Ethics* 20 (1994), 67.

Steve Jones, *The Language of the Genes: Biology, History and the Evolutionary Future* (London: HarperCollins, 1993).

Steve Jones, *In the Blood: God, Genes and Destiny* (London: HarperCollins, 1996).

Bernard Hoose, 'Genetic engineering: the new revolution', *The Month,* June 1991, 240- 244.

Robin McKie, *The Genetic Jigsaw: The Story of the New Genetics* (Oxford: OUP, 1988).

Nuffield Council on Bioethics, *Genetic Screening: Ethical Issues,* London, 1993.

Johannes Relter, 'Genetic Therapy and Ethics', *Theology Digest,* 1986, 245-250.

Report of the Committee on the Ethics of Gene Therapy, presented to the British Parliament, January 1992.

John Scally (ed.), *Ethics in Crisis?* (Dublin: Veritas, 1997).

Paul Schotsmans, 'The Genetic Challenge to Ethics', *Concilium,* n.203, 1992, pp 89-104.

Mary J. Seller, 'Genetic Counselling' in *Principles of Health Care Ethics,* Raanan Gillon (ed.) (London: SCM, 1994).

David Smith, *Life and Morality* (Dublin: Gill & Macmillan, 1995).

World Council of Churches, *Biotechnology: Its Challenges to the Churches and the World,* 1989.

Noam J. Zohar, 'Can a person benefit from being altered?', *Bioethics,* 5 (1991), 275-288.